THE JERRY TWOMEY

COLLECTION

at The Winnipeg Art Gallery:

Inuit Sculpture from the Canadian Arctic

Curated by Darlene Coward Wight

THE WINNIPEG ART GALLERY

Jerry Twomey in the Inuit vault at The Winnipeg Art Gallery, September 2003.

Catalogue of the exhibition *The Jerry Twomey Collection at The Winnipeg Art Gallery: Inuit Sculpture from the Canadian Arctic* organized by The Winnipeg Art Gallery and presented May 8, 2003 to March 10, 2004.

National Library of Canada Cataloguing in Publication Data

Winnipeg Art Gallery
The Jerry Twomey Collection at The Winnipeg Art Gallery: Inuit Sculpture from the Canadian Arctic / Darlene Coward Wight

Includes bibliographical references and index.
Catalogue of an exhibition held at the Winnipeg Art Gallery.

ISBN 0-88915-223-3

1. Inuit sculpture—Canada—Exhibitions. 2. Twomey, Jerry—
Art collections—Exhibitions. 3. Winnipeg Art Gallery—
Exhibitions. 4. Sculpture—Manitoba—Winnipeg—Exhibitions.
I. Wight, Darlene. II. Title.
E99.E7W72 2003   730'.89'9712   C2003-910628-4

Cover image: **JOANASEE KAKKIK**, *Man and Woman* (detail), c. 1969

CONTENTS

Director's Preface

JERRY F. TWOMEY BOUGHT HIS FIRST THREE INUIT CARVINGS
for $8.00 in 1952 from the Hudson's Bay Company in Winnipeg. By 1971 he was
an internationally known plant breeder and geneticist, and had collected close to
4,000 Inuit sculptures. Retirement and a new life in the San Diego area meant
the need for a new home for his collection. In spite of mounting pressure from
museums in a number of European countries and in the U.S., as well as from
private dealers and collectors, Twomey was determined that his unique
collection should remain in Canada, preferably in Winnipeg.

This dream was realized when the Secretary of State in Ottawa and the Province
of Manitoba both announced financial assistance to purchase the collection.
Twomey made a significant donation as well. The 3,900-piece collection was
transferred from the Twomey home to the newly constructed Winnipeg Art
Gallery in 1971.

Jerry Twomey was the first collector to research the individual artists who
were creating sculpture in the 1950s and 1960s. He exhaustively classified and
physically organized his collection by community and artist, identifying artists
by family group. In order to determine the most talented artists carving at that
time, he bought from literally every dealer and wholesale agency in the country.
His collection included carvings from every art-producing community at that
time—30 in all.

The Jerry Twomey Collection is a definitive overview of Inuit carving activity
across the Canadian Arctic in the first two decades that Inuit sculpture was
marketed in Southern Canada. This exhibition is a tribute to the vision and
dedication of the man who collected the art.

I would like to thank Friesens Corporation and the Volunteer Committee to The
Winnipeg Art Gallery for their sponsorship of this exhibition and publication.

Patricia E. Bovey
Director

Sculpture organized by artist on shelves in the Twomey home at Lyndale Drive, Winnipeg, 1971.

DARLENE COWARD WIGHT

Introduction

THE JERRY TWOMEY COLLECTION OF 3,900 SCULPTURES has been a key source for exhibitions at The Winnipeg Art Gallery since it was acquired in 1971. No matter what the theme or focus of the show, there have usually been Twomey pieces included. I met Jerry Twomey for the first time in November 1987 when he paid an unexpected visit to the Gallery. It occurred to me at that time that I knew very little about this collector who was omnipresent for me and my work. When he reappeared again with no notice ten years later, in April 1997, I did my first taped interview. I was fascinated to hear some of the stories about his scientific background and how he collected portions of his collection. In 1972, a small "Selections" show had been organized by Jacqueline Fry, part-time Curator of Non-Western Art for the Gallery. It was accompanied by a 10-page brochure that served as a brief introduction to the collection. Nothing has been published since then. I determined that it was essential to learn more about Jerry Twomey and to document the important collection he created. Two essays follow: biographical information and a description of Twomey's collecting activities, based on taped interviews done in Winnipeg from 1999 to 2002, and a second text outlining the acquisition and cataloguing of his collection by the Gallery from 1969 to 1975.

The exhibition is organized to reflect the interests of and original research by Jerry Twomey. He was the first collector to meticulously document the pieces that he collected. Carvings were organized on shelves and on every available surface throughout his house and garage according to community of origin, artist, and family relationships. Triangular wooden tags were placed on the shelves identifying artists, and many of these tags are still in use today in the Gallery's Inuit vault. They are in the following coded form:

> E7-1168 [disc number]
> Pootoogook, Kananginak [artist's surname, first name]
> C.D. F78, H, 35 [Cape Dorset, Family 78, Husband, Born in 1935]

Twomey collected carvings from virtually every Inuit community producing art in the 1950s and 1960s. A complete listing of his collection at The Winnipeg Art Gallery is given in a table at the back of this catalogue. It is organized alphabetically by community and by artist, and includes the total number of carvings by each artist. Such a large sampling allows insights into which artists were actively creating carvings in these two decades. A second list provides an alphabetical index of artists in the exhibition.

The exhibition is organized by region, community, and artist. The regions of Nunavik (Arctic Quebec), Qikiqtaalik (Baffin), and Kivalliq (Keewatin) are represented. As revealed by the listing for the whole Twomey Collection, there are also pieces from Kitikmeot communities, but the numbers are low and so are not represented in the exhibition. The catalogue of sculpture from each of the three regions is preceded by an introduction to the history and art activities of each community in the 1950s and 1960s. An overview of the Twomey Collection is provided for each community. As other authors have written about the art of many of the communities, a bibliography is provided at the end of each section to facilitate further research.

Pieces for inclusion in the exhibition were chosen with the following criteria in mind:

■ aesthetic quality (including craftsmanship, uniqueness, inventive use of carving material)
■ unique or unusual pieces that expand current knowledge of an artist's oeuvre
■ numbers of carvings from each community in proportion to the overall collection.

The exhibition has afforded an opportunity to make use of research that was not available when the collection was initially catalogued from May 1972 to September 1975. More information is now available about artists, allowing further identifications and attributions. In true scientific fashion, when he purchased the majority of his pieces, Twomey filled out index cards to which he attached tags or labels. These cards came to the Gallery with the collection, and information on these cards usually includes inventory numbers from source Arctic co-operatives. During my research, it was discovered that these numbers were sometimes coded with the date of purchase by the co-operative. The most exciting discovery was "cracking" the code for Repulse Bay, giving dates for literally hundreds of previously undated carvings.

While the exhibition and catalogue focus on contemporary carvings by Canadian Inuit artists, there are other portions of Twomey's collection that must be mentioned. An ivory tupilak from Angmassalik dating to c. 1850 and three dolls are from Greenland. A group of 91 ivory carvings were purchased from the widow of Bishop Archibald Lang Fleming. These may have been collected while "the flying bishop" lived at Lake Harbour (now Kimmirut) from 1909 to 1916, where he established an Anglican mission. They are small models of tools and weapons, and utilitarian objects such as buttons and even crochet hooks. Two miniature animals are from Alaska. Another five Alaskan pieces were collected by Twomey from other sources, including noted art historian for Alaska, Dorothy Jean Ray.

A group of 48 prehistoric objects was purchased by Twomey in 1961 from Park Lane Antiques, a shop that he frequented in Vancouver. A letter of provenance states that the artifacts were from the collection of Alfred H. Anderson, who "is known for his work with the Eskimos, and he excavated an ancient village on Point Crusenstern, Coronation Gulf Region." This is probably a reference to Cape Krusenstern, a point of land on the northwest shore of the Coronation Gulf, north of the present-day community of Kugluktuk (formerly Coppermine). The objects include labrets, and if they were from that location originally, it would mean that the male practice of wearing labrets (studs or button-like facial decorations inserted into the lower lip) was carried on farther east than has been believed.[1]

The remainder of the collection, 3,757 pieces, are by Canadian Inuit carvers and date from 1952 to 1970. The earliest dated piece is from 1954, but some of the carvings Twomey purchased in the early 1950s were not dated. For many of the communities, it is possible to see the beginnings of artistic development and for some, such as Baker Lake, Arviat, Repulse Bay, Rankin Inlet, Cape Dorset, and Inukjuak, there are large enough numbers spread over several years to detect changes in style and carving stone. It is hoped that the sample included in this publication will provide some insights into the creativity that was evident in the Canadian Arctic at a time when few people were collecting. It is a tribute to the foresight of a collector who never doubted that the art he was collecting should one day be a worthy part of our Canadian heritage. ■

1. See William Healey Dall. *Report of the Bureau of Ethnology, Smithsonian Institution, on Masks, Labrets, and Certain Other Aboriginal Customs, with an inquiry into the bearing of their geographical distribution.* No. 3, 1881-82, p. 77-157. It was believed that the practice of "labretifery" extended no further east than Cape Bathurst, west of Paulatuk.

The Collector

JEREMIAH FORSTER TWOMEY WAS BORN ON SEPTEMBER 11, 1915 in Camrose, Alberta, the eldest of nine children. He was named after his father, whose family was from Ireland originally. His mother was Olga Elizabeth Forster, of Austrian descent. His father resigned his post at St. Michael's College in Toronto and moved the family to Camrose to manage the family coal mine near the town.[1] An aunt, Genevieve Twomey, taught art and became head of the Art Department at the University of Alberta. She was later involved in the founding of the Banff School of Fine Art.

After 14 years in Camrose, the family moved to Winnipeg in 1928. Jerry Twomey attended high school at St Paul's College in Selkirk. He received his Bachelor of Science and Agriculture degree from the University of Manitoba, with a major in genetics. From his early high school days, he was intrigued by hybridization, and at the age of 15, he began breeding gladioli. He discovered that the chromosomes of gladioli could be mutated by subjecting them to X-rays. One of his professors was so impressed with the young man's findings that he arranged for him to use the X-ray equipment at Winnipeg's General Hospital for his flower experiments. With the help of an English gardener, he experimented in the greenhouse at Pound's, a Winnipeg florist, and succeeded, at the age of 24, in producing a new gladiolus with eight petals.[2] Persistent breeding produced a vigorous pure white glad with a scarlet blotch. He named it after his grandmother, Margaret Beaton, and the flower won "World's Most Beautiful Glad" at the 1939 World's Fair in New York. The prize of $10,000 was generous during the Depression.

Post-graduate studies in taxonomy and genetics at the University of Minnesota in 1935-36 resulted in a Master's degree. He continued his post-graduate studies and had completed all of the course work for a doctorate when his studies were interrupted by World War II. He became associated with McFayden Seeds in the early 1930s, then Canada's largest mail-order seed company. During the war, he worked for the federal Department of Agriculture to develop seeds for the Allies.

In 1946 Twomey and his brother Patrick (Paddy) started a mail-order seed company, T & T Seeds, on Lombard Street in Winnipeg. In 1967 he gave his share of the company to Paddy. Today it is owned by his nephews, Kevin (who took over its management in the late 1980s) and Brian. In 1997 T & T Seeds moved to its current expanded facilities and greenhouses in Headingley. Today it is one of the five largest mail-order garden suppliers in Canada and sends out 200,000 catalogues internationally.

1. Twomey's father and mother passed away in 1978 and 1988 respectively.

2. From the 1930s to the 1960s, glads were the most popular hobby flower and outsold roses in florists' shops.

In the early 1950s, dwarf, rust-resistant wheat varieties, with their exceptionally high yields, began to interest Twomey. After a number of years of research and field trips all over the world, he worked with such scientists and fellow plant breeders as Dr. Norm Borlaug, Nobel-prize winner for his wheat research; Alfedo Garcia; Jacobo Ortega; and Frank Peto. In 1960 Twomey and a number of other plant breeders and geneticists formed an international private seed company, World Seeds. Sales were slow so they marketed their seed in Russia. For the next ten years sales of seed to Russia were brisk. These activities meant several trips to Russia at a time when few others had that opportunity.[3]

Throughout much of his career, Twomey had travelled to California frequently. In the late 1960s he decided to retire from the seed business, move to California, and, at the age of 55, to begin a new interest—breeding roses. As he had always planned on his Inuit sculpture collection going to a Canadian museum, the time had come for this to happen. He engaged the services of Toronto dealer Av Isaacs to handle the sale/donation of his collection, and moved to the San Diego area of California where he claims the climate is perfect for roses. In 1981 he met Lawrence Smith, a noted California rosarian, who became Twomey's mentor. Rather than breeding for larger and showier blooms, he recognized that gardeners would appreciate a rose that could be grown easily and without the use of chemicals.

By the early 1990s unprecedented success was achieved in the form of international recognition for his roses. In 1991 he won the All-American Rose Selection (AARS) award for a rose, "Sheer Elegance." In 1992 he won the same award for a second year in a row for "All That Jazz," which won for vigour and disease resistance. Twomey was one of only two amateur breeders in 50 years to win the world's most prestigious honour given for roses.[4] In 1993 he won an international prize, the Gold Medal, at The Hague for a rose he named in memory of Dutch-born actress Audrey Hepburn.

At the age of 88, Twomey is still actively breeding roses. He has seedlings that will soon be available for Canadian gardeners.

COLLECTING ACTIVITIES

Jerry Twomey traces his childhood interest in Inuit carving to his cousin, Arthur Twomey, who became a noted ornithologist with a specialization in Arctic birds. The two boys grew up in Camrose, Alberta. Arthur became interested in collecting and stuffing birds from a naturalist in Camrose, Frank Mowat, the great-uncle of writer Farley Mowat. He pursued his interest by earning a Bachelor degree in ornithology at the University of Alberta and doing post-graduate work in Urbana, Illinois. He travelled to the Canadian Arctic over several years doing research for his doctoral thesis and, later on, for the Carnegie Museum in Pittsburgh. He visited the Twomey home in Winnipeg on his way home from the Arctic, and told stories of living and travelling with Inuit, for whom he had a great admiration. When Jerry Twomey saw his first Inuit carvings, "I had a warm and curious background of appreciation for these enterprising, imaginative, and long-surviving people."[5]

Twomey saw his first carvings in the Hudson's Bay Company store in Winnipeg in 1952. There were three or four tables of small, grey pieces, priced $2-$5 each and he bought three for $8. The Winnipeg branch of the Canadian Guild of Crafts also began to retail carvings in March 1952.[6] Twomey became a friend of Bessie Bulman, Director of the Guild in Winnipeg. He would try to be present to get first pick when exhibitions opened. As his own profession came to demand more of his time, he asked bush pilots, prospectors, reporters, and missionaries to buy carvings for him. "Many of the carvings I got in this manner were not at all what I wanted, so after systematic selection I traded them to dealers or gave them away as gifts."[7]

Twomey's training as a biologist and his study of taxonomy, the classification of plants, influenced his collecting:

Horticulturally, for breeding a crop you have to get a cross-section back to the species to see what is there to build upon, disease resistance, health, and so forth. You have to get a broad look. So I collected taxonomically to find out who the

3. It was Twomey's contacts in Russia who helped the important *Sculpture/Inuit* touring exhibition to visit two venues, Moscow and Leningrad in 1971/72.

4. See Hurney article.

5. WAG Education department brochure, 1974.

6. Wight, *The First Passionate Collector*, 72.

7. Secretary of State News Release, June 5, 1972.

artists were. You soon found out there were 2 or 3 artists in each community and you began looking for their carvings. It wasn't long before I was buying in quantity. If you didn't buy something at the time, you would probably never see it again. I had post-dated cheques from one end of the country to the other. Every time I got into a bad business deal, I'd go out and buy more carvings so I'd have to go back to work! My poor wife would say, "What are you doing with more carvings!" We already had a basement full. I had a garage attached to the house, and a basement under that, built to grow tulips. It was soon full of carvings on shelves that I built. Then I parked the car outside the garage and filled that with carvings. I had them organized by area and artist right from the beginning. I was brainwashed in genetics. [8]

This taxonomy approach to collecting was particularly relevant to the massive number of carvings (1,669) he acquired from Repulse Bay. The small sizes and low prices made this possible. "Price was a factor. If you are trying to get a cross-section of who the artists are, the more you could accumulate, the better. In the beginning when I started collecting I wasn't that disciplined. Until George [Swinton] smartened me up as to what good primitive art was. I think there was a lot of Repulse Bay coming down at the beginning. More so than the other areas."

Twomey's interest in the artists and families of Repulse Bay is reflected in a group of photographs he took in the community during a trip there in the 1960s (see Kivalliq section). Each photograph is carefully documented with the name of every man, woman, and child in the family groupings. He was particularly pleased to meet John Kaunak and his family, as he had been collecting Kaunak's work intensively. He made 8 to 10 trips to the Arctic in the 1950s and 1960s, often accompanying Ron Milligan from the Department of Indian and Northern Affairs. "I suppose I made a half-dozen trips with Milligan. In the early days I'd have pots of daffodils and tulips blooming in my basement. I'd put them in polyethylene bags and go up to Churchill with a couple of dozen pots to give as gifts." He visited Kivalliq communities on the west side of Hudson Bay (see Arviat photographs) and several Nunavik communities on the east coast, including Puvirnituq,

where he was able to commission realistic bird carvings from two artists, Aisapik Quma Igauja and Samisa Passauralu Ivilla (see Puvirnituq). For Twomey these trips were important opportunities to meet the carvers, and he documented some of them with photographs that have been included in the community sections of this catalogue.

Twomey credits George Swinton for broadening his artistic tastes. "In the beginning I was buying realistic carvings and bypassing the very primitive, unfinished ones. George said, 'When you look at a realistic carving, you see it all and you tire of it quickly. You don't look at it again.' We had fun! I was privileged to see the carvings through George's eyes, as well as appreciate the things as I saw them. I made a quiet deal with George. I would buy the big carvings and he would take the small things. He could then sneak them into his house without his wife, Alice, seeing them. They would end up in the attic, but she would find them." The two men did much trading back and forth as they defined and refined their personal preferences and interests.

George Swinton had moved to Winnipeg in 1954 to take a job teaching in the School of Art at the University of Manitoba. The two men met in the mid-1950s through Cecil Stewart of the Hudson's Bay Company. Stewart had helped Twomey amass a small collection of Inuit carvings by that time and he wanted to know what a group of university professors would think of them. He invited the professors to visit the basement of Twomey's house, where the carvings were stored on shelves.[9] Swinton was one of the group and he was most impressed by what he saw. The two men became close friends and generously helped each other in their mutual collecting activities over the years. Swinton helped Twomey with his artist's eye and Twomey's incredible zeal in acquiring carvings by the hundreds must have been of great educational value to Swinton.

Swinton's daughter, Nelda, remembers Twomey well:

I have great recollections of Jerry arriving quite often to our house with cigar in hand. When my mother wasn't home, the cigar would enter the house. Otherwise, it was

8. All quotes by Twomey are from various taped interviews done in Winnipeg in 1999, 2002, and 2003.

9. Twomey explained: "When the Hudson's Bay Company hired a new Scotsman they'd bring them over to my basement to show them what good carvings looked like. They could see a cross-section of carving from a particular area that they were going to. They could say, this is a good one and this is junk. It upgraded the purchasing."

Sculpture in living room of Twomey house, 1971

kept on the front porch, waiting for a ride back home with Jerry ... . You could always tell if Jerry had been over, for the house or front porch usually smelled of cigar. As soon as Jerry arrived he would automatically run up two flights of stairs to talk and discuss art and life (I suppose) with George. They would spend hours talking, however, I do not believe Moira or I ever listened in on a conversation. They enjoyed a drink or two, but never overindulged in the alcohol. When we went to the Twomey house in the summertime, Jerry would bring us out to his garden and show us his prized gladioli. He was a connoisseur of flowers, in particular those gladioli. We even went to see the botanical exhibitions where his flowers were on display. I remember his basement full of shelves with hundreds of Inuit sculptures and thought he was a real collector. I was overwhelmed by the massiveness of his collection. He was always kind, polite, and funny and I loved the way he said George's name ... . Oh come on Geoorrge ... .[10]

In the early 1960s, the two collectors came to the conclusion that a book should be published about the art. Swinton was a writer as well as an artist and was willing to take on this job. Twomey brought his entrepreneurial spirit to the challenge of finding a publisher for the proposed book. "We tried the government, publishers, everybody! I knew a fellow in Seattle who was publishing books about hobbies. I asked him if he would publish a book on Eskimo carving, and he said 'Hell, yes!' So George and I went out to Seattle. We came back and passed the word around that a book about Canadian Inuit sculpture was going to be published in Seattle. It wasn't long before McClelland and Stewart in Toronto agreed to publish the book."[11]

Twomey's collecting was aided by the travelling he did for various seed companies. "I was travelling back and forth to California frequently. I could buy a plane ticket in California, and for $20 to $25 more I could go home by way of Montreal. I would drop in at the Canadian Handicrafts Guild, then stop in Toronto, visit a brother in Niagara Falls, and return to Winnipeg for little extra cost. I made that route two

or three times a year, at least. The Guild in Montreal and Winnipeg were great sources of carvings. Toronto not so much."

Twomey collected works by southern Canadian artists with some enthusiasm as well:

I got to know artists around Vancouver: Jack Shadbolt, Joe Plaskett, Smith. They were all poor. I would go to Alvin Balkin's gallery down from the Georgia Hotel that was a kind of meeting place. Artists would bring in their pictures. I bought Shadbolt's watercolours for $50 to $75. I got to know Joe Plaskett well, and used to visit him in Paris ... . I'd buy 10 to 20 pastels at a time. Maybe some oils. Then I had to sell them to my brothers to pay for the Eskimo carvings. Group of Seven works were very cheap. I was in Vancouver once and telephoned Mrs. [Lawren] Harris and said I loved the work her husband was doing. I had heard he had some sketches and would he be willing to sell any? She laughed and said she would tell Lawren to bring some down to the gallery. He came with 4 or 5 Lake Superior oil sketches (8" x 12"). I think I bought 2 of them for $160. Now they're $10,000 apiece. My definition of intelligence is recognizing the obvious just a little ahead of the other guy. [Eskimo] carvings that I paid $80 to $100 for are now $5,000 to $10,000. It was so cheap and so obvious! I couldn't resist it.

The collecting did not stop after Twomey moved to California. For ten years he collected woodcarvings by the Sari Indians who live on the Gulf of Mexico. He still has 200 to 300 carvings in storage. ■

BIOGRAPHY SOURCES

Hurney, Jeanne Muraco. "'All That Jazz', Flaunting Convention, Amateur Breeds Roses for the 90s Gardener." *American Association of Retired Persons* (July/August 1992): 20.

Sinclair, Gordon Jr. "The Budding Genius." *Winnipeg Homes* (Fall 1997): 101.

Streeper, Dick. "Sweet Dreams." *The San Diego Union-Tribune* (April 16, 2000): H15, H20.

10. Written communication, October 15, 2003.

11. This is in reference to George Swinton's first book, *Eskimo Sculpture/Sculpture Esquimaude*, published in 1965.

The Twomey Collection

at The Winnipeg Art Gallery

THROUGHOUT HIS YEARS OF COLLECTING INUIT SCULPTURE, Jerry Twomey had always planned that his collection would end up in a public art gallery. He gives credit for this goal to Cecil Stewart, who worked for the Hudson's Bay Company in Winnipeg for many of Twomey's collecting years. Stewart had an appreciation for the carvings that arrived at the Hudson's Bay Company warehouse from communities across the Canadian Arctic. He agreed to assist Jerry Twomey and George Swinton by notifying them when notable or requested carvings arrived from the North, on the understanding that the work would eventually go to a Canadian museum. The help he gave the two collectors was invaluable. Ron Milligan was a federal development officer who became a friend of Twomey and took him along on several trips to Arctic communities.

When Twomey made the decision to retire and move to the San Diego area of California, negotiations began with The Winnipeg Art Gallery. His collecting activities were well-known by then and he was approached by a number of collectors, dealers, and museums anxious to acquire his holdings. On December 26, 1969, Twomey visited the home of Ferdinand Eckhardt, then Director of The Winnipeg Art Gallery, to discuss the long-term loan of his collection to the Gallery when the Gallery's new building was completed.[1] Discussions soon involved a more permanent transfer to the Gallery—the purchase of the collection.

A force behind the negotiations was the Assistant Deputy Minister of Tourism, Recreation, and Culture for Manitoba, Mary Elizabeth Bayer. Edward Schreyer was Premier at the time. On August 25, 1971, a special warrant authorizing the purchase of this "national treasure" was passed by the provincial cabinet and announced by Cultural Affairs Minister Peter Burtniak. A two-third's share of the collection was purchased for $185,000 with an option to buy the remaining third as funds became available. In a letter from Bayer to Eckhardt on September 9, 1971 giving formal notification of the purchase, Bayer states: "While the financial arrangements are being worked out, we will be able to take over the entire collection ... . We look forward to seeing it on display as soon as possible ... . We would hope that Professor Swinton will be asked to serve as a consultant in the cataloguing and exhibiting of these important works."

When the new Gallery building at 300 Memorial Boulevard opened on September 25, 1971, 14 pieces were borrowed from the Twomey home for a one-day display. But the public was given its first real glimpse at the collection in

1. Memo from Ferdinand Eckhardt, December 31, 1969.

*Marsha Twomey, Byron MacLellan, and Lee Saidman cataloguing
Twomey Collection at The Winnipeg Art Gallery.*

1. Memo from Ferdinand
Eckhardt, December 31, 1969.
The new Gallery building at 300
Memorial Boulevard was officially
opened on September 25, 1971.

2. Press Release, April 3, 1972.

3. Twomey made a donation of
$50,000.

4. Press Release for Festival/
Manitoba, June 12, 1972.

5. See Bibliographies for each
region.

February-March 1972 when 58 sculptures were
exhibited in *Selections from the Twomey Collection*,
accompanied by a 10-page brochure prepared by
curator Jacqueline Fry.

On March 28, 1972, a new national policy for
museums was announced by Secretary of State,
Gérard Pelletier. There were two main themes:

*One is concerned with retaining those things important to
our national heritage and conserving them for future
generations. The other aims to decentralize museum services
to communities across the country so that the enjoyment and
study of these cultural treasures does not remain concentrated
in the large museums of a few major metropolitan centres.*

*During the first year the policy is in effect, the federal
government is devoting $9,400,000 to launch programs
designed to attain these goals.*

This new policy had a direct impact on the Twomey
Collection. On June 5, 1972, James Richardson,
Minister of Supply and Services, made the following
announcement in a State Department news release:

*The federal government has joined Manitoba in acquiring
the renowned collection of Eskimo sculpture and artifacts
brought together over a span of two decades by the
Winnipeg scientist and businessman, Jerry Twomey.*

*Mr. Richardson met Mr. L. Desjardins, the Manitoba
Minister of Tourism, Recreation and Cultural Affairs, at
the Winnipeg Art Gallery today to present the federal
government's contribution of $75,000.*

*The Ottawa share of the purchase comes from the
Department of the Secretary of State whose new national
museums policy focuses on retaining recognized national
treasures in Canada and on developing regional and local
museum resources. Manitoba's share of $150,000 [sic] was
made public some time ago.*

*The Twomey collection was offered on the art market last
fall and bids to purchase were received from collectors in
other countries as well as Canada. In this situation, as
Mr. Richardson explained it, "We were anxious to keep the
collection in Canada, and to keep it intact, as an inheritance
for our people."*

*Mr. L. Desjardins added, "Mr. Twomey was willing to
contribute a substantial portion of the collection as a gift to
the people of this province.*[3] *It was a unique, once-in-a-life-
time opportunity and we were delighted with this decision
by the federal government to share in this acquisition."*

Transfer of the 3,900 carvings from the Twomey
home on Lyndale Drive to the Gallery began in
mid-April, 1972, and was completed 3½ months later,
on June 29. A grant was received from the Provincial
government to hire two people to catalogue the
collection. Marsha Twomey, Jerry Twomey's daughter,
and Byron MacLellan, who had lived in Kuujuaraapik
for two years, began work on May 15, 1972. Cataloguing
was not completed until early September 1975.

The cataloguing process became the subject of public
programming in the summer of 1972. Every Thursday
and Friday afternoon, from 2:00pm to 5:00pm, the
public could view "the actual cataloguing, restoration,
and repairing processes involved ... throughout the
summer."[4] The press release quoted George Swinton's
appraisal of the Twomey collection as "not only the
largest collection of its kind but also the only
collection with any kind of coherence and historical
completeness. The collection is unique in that it
shows the artistic development, increasing skills,
and trends of subject matter of the [Inuit] people."

Another activity that took place in the summer of 1972 was the photographing of all 3,900 carvings in the collection by Steven Nuytten and Neil Sandell. These black-and-white photographs remain a valuable source of documentation of the collection.

Exhibition of the Twomey Collection has been ongoing over the years. Twenty-seven sculptures were included in the landmark *Sculpture/Inuit* exhibition organized in 1971 by the Canadian Eskimo Arts Council. This exhibition toured extensively to Moscow, Leningrad, Copenhagen, Paris, London, Philadelphia, Ottawa, and Vancouver, and played an important role in raising international awareness of the artform. In May 1979, 37 Twomey pieces were displayed at UNESCO, Place de Fontenoy, Paris, as part of a cultural event called Canada Days. Significant numbers of works were included in each of the eight "Settlement Series" catalogues published by The Winnipeg Art Gallery from 1976 to 1983.[5] Given the vast scope of the collection, and The Winnipeg Art Gallery's ongoing policy of exhibiting its permanent collection of art by Inuit, sculpture from the Twomey Collection will continue to play an important role in revealing themes, stylistic developments, important artists, and many other intellectual and visual facets of Inuit creativity. ■

SOURCES/SELECTED READING

The Beaver. "The Artists of Arctic Bay." (Autumn, 1967).

Fry, Jacqueline. *Eskimo Sculpture: Selections from the Twomey Collection*. Winnipeg: The Winnipeg Art Gallery, February-March, 1972.

Graham, John W. "Eskimo Sculpture is 'Incomparable'." *Winnipeg Free Press*, March 1, 1972. (Review of Twomey exhibition)

Secretary of State News Release. "New National Policy for Museums." Release No. 4-372E. April 3, 1972.

Secretary of State News Release. "Ottawa Joins Manitoba to Complete Purchase of Twomey Collection." June 5, 1972.

Secretary of State News Release. "The Twomey Collection." June 5, 1972.

Secretary of State News Release. "The Twomey Collection: How a plant breeder developed a fine collection of Eskimo art." June 5, 1972.

Star & Times. "Eskimo Art Collection Purchased by Province." September 23, 1971.

Tribune. "Province to purchase part of Eskimo art collection." August 30, 1971.

Tribune. "Ottawa helps buy Eskimo art." June 7, 1972.

van Rijn, Nick. "Private 'mania' for Eskimo art leads to public collection." *Tribune*, June 17, 1972.

Viewpoint. "Ottawa joins Manitoba to complete purchase of Twomey collection." June 14, 1972.

Nunavik Region

ON NOVEMBER 11, 1975, THE JAMES BAY AND NORTHERN QUÉBEC Agreement (JBNQA) was signed, settling issues of land ownership and allowing the James Bay hydro project to proceed. It did not result in self-government for the Inuit of Nunavik (Northern Québec) or the creation of a new territory as in Nunavut. The JBNQA is administered by Makivik, an Inuit-owned economic development corporation formed in 1978.

INUKJUAK

The year 1949 is now considered the beginning of the contemporary period of Inuit art, as it marked the beginning of the continuing creation of art and craft items for export to southern markets. James Houston first purchased carvings in Inukjuak (formerly Port Harrison) in 1949 for an historic sales exhibition at the Canadian Guild of Crafts Québec in Montréal.[1] A marble-like, olive green stone, sometimes with gold streaks, was available for carving in the early 1950s. Contrasting materials such as ivory, bone, light coloured stone, even soap and plastic, were used to inlay eyes, faces, and other details in stone sculptures. Subjects usually depicted animals and everyday life in winter and summer hunting camps. Carvings were purchased for the Guild by the Hudson's Bay Company, which had maintained a post in the area since 1921. In 1965 a co-operative store was opened, and has been a support to carvers over the years.

Jerry Twomey collected 175 sculptures from Inukjuak, by 66 known and 19 unknown artists. Of particular interest is a classically beautiful head of a woman by Abraham Nastapoka that makes stunning use of the Inukjuak stone. This sculpture reflects a tendency among Inukjuak carvers to create round, smooth surfaces that show the stone to best advantage.

PUVIRNITUQ

James Houston returned to the Arctic in 1950 and visited Puvirnituq (formerly Povungnituk) as well as Inukjuak to make further purchases for a second Guild exhibition. Sales were brisk and Inuit sculpture was firmly launched onto the international art market. Sculpture from Puvirnituq is characterized by intricate detail and smooth, glossy surfaces. The stone is grey, but usually polished. As in Inukjuak, subjects are realistic and often depict domestic life and animals. However,

1. See Wight, *The First Passionate Collector*, 1990, 45-92.

a small group of artists in Puvirnituq have become known for "fantastic" spirit images, and Twomey collected several imaginative examples of this genre, such as a frog-like *Spirit* by Eli Sallualu Qinuajua.[2]

Carving has remained an important industry in Puvirnituq over the years. In 1951 the Hudson's Bay Company opened a general store and purchased carvings on an ongoing basis. In 1956 a Catholic mission was founded and two years later Father André Steinmann encouraged residents to form the Carvers Association of Povungnituk, the first organization of its kind in the Canadian Arctic. In 1961 this Association became the Co-operative Association of Povungnituk. Today it remains one of the most active of the co-operatives that make up La Fédération des Co-opératives du Nouveau-Québec, formed in 1967.

Twomey collected 120 sculptures by 48 known and 8 unknown artists from Puvirnituq from the mid-1950s to the late 1960s. There are two special groups of highly detailed carvings of birds by Puvirnituq artists in the Twomey Collection that deserve special note. Twomey visited the community about 1960 and commissioned the carvings from two Puvirnituq artists, Aisapik Quma Igauja and Samisa Passauralu Ivilla. Ten bird carvings were purchased from Samisa in February 1961, as documented by a list Twomey compiled at the time. That indicates they were created in 1960. At least ten carvings by Aisapik are on another list of received items for fall 1961. It can probably be assumed that the bird carvings by that artist were made in 1961. Twomey remembers that a missionary living in Puvirnituq at the time facilitated the commission of these works.

Also of special note for Puvirnituq are the major pieces by Davidialuk Alasua Amittu and Joe Talirunili. One of the most unique pieces in the entire WAG Collection is Davidialuk's so-called *Mythological Bird*. It is unusual within the artist's oeuvre for its size and subject matter. A female shaman transforms into an eagle, not in itself unusual, but the formal and symmetrical composition is monumental in its visual impact. The figure is divided vertically with human arm, breast and leg

on the left side, and bird body on the right. Twomey enjoys telling the story of how he acquired the work. One Saturday morning in 1958, he was telephoned by Hudson's Bay Company employee Cecil Stewart. Stewart told him that a piece had just arrived at the warehouse that Twomey should buy, as it had to end up in a museum. This was a reference to the agreement between them that the final destination of Twomey's collection would be a public museum. Twomey rushed to the warehouse and bought the sculpture with a post-dated cheque for $100, as he was over-extended financially at the time.

Joe Talirunili created numerous examples of his *Migration* boats over his creative life, and Twomey collected a very fine example in c. 1965. Much more unusual for this artist is a large 1959 sculpture of an Inuk dragging a huge arm. This might have an autobiographical reference to a gun accident that occurred in 1950. Talirunili's father was cleaning his gun when it discharged and hit the artist in the shoulder. Talirunili has described his memories of this event in Myers, *Joe Talirunili*: "I looked and I could see my arm which was far away. It was just attached to me by three pieces of skin."

SALLUIT

Prompted by the success of Guild sales of carvings from Inukjuak and Puvirnituq, the Hudson's Bay Company began to buy carvings from Salluit (formerly Sugluk and Saglouc) carvers in 1952. Jim Haining organized the quarrying of stone from the Kovic River Valley and sold it to carvers at cost—50 cents a pound. Work was displayed in the company store as an encouragement to others. Production increased and by 1956 half the total income of the community came from the sale of carvings. Souvenir items were discouraged and quality carvings were received with enthusiasm in this period of the mid-1950s. The result was a creative outpouring of original work in the light grey Kovic River stone, created without outside stylistic influence.[4] However, in 1957 the Hudson's Bay Company interpreted a decline in sales as consumer resistance to the unpolished grey carving stone, and buying was halted. This, combined with a declining

2. A carving competition was organized in Puvirnituq in 1967 by anthropologist Nelson Graburn that challenged artists to create new thoughts, or pieces from their imaginations. It inspired the production of a large number of carvings depicting composite and spirit beings. Some of these were featured in an exhibition organized by George Swinton in 1972. (See Swinton, *Eskimo Fantastic Art*, 1972)

3. Myers, 1977, 20.

4. Roberts, 1977, 14.

supply of stone at local quarry sites, resulted in a diminished enthusiasm among carvers for creating quality sculptures. The subsequent arrival of government buyers, and renewed interest by the Hudson's Bay Company, were not sufficient incentive to restore creative energies to the level of the early period of 1952-1957.[5]

Twomey collected 61 carvings by 31 known and 16 unknown Salluit artists. There are several major works, including *Mother and Girl* by Mary Irqiquq Sorusiluk, *Woman Removing Child from Amautik* by Maggie Ittuvik Tayarak, and the unusual *Smoking Mother with Child* by Tivi Ilisituk. Two of these important works are by female carvers, revealing an interesting distinction from other Nunavik communities. Research for an exhibition in 1990, *Women and Art in Salluit: The Poetry of the Early Sculpture*, revealed this fact. When a selection for the exhibition was made from The Winnipeg Art Gallery's 124 Salluit sculptures on a purely aesthetic basis, it was discovered that, with very few exceptions, the works depicted women. Further research revealed that 15 of the 18 identified artists represented in the final selection of 42 works were women.

This finding was surprising in relation to the dominant number of male carvers in other prolific communities in the 1950s—Inukjuak, Puvirnituq, and Cape Dorset. In interviews with Nelson Graburn, all but one of the male Salluit carvers said they "loathed" the activity and would much rather go hunting.[6] Another answer might lie in the strong tradition of doll-making by the women of Nunavik. The single, frontal figures in stone are often similar in pose to the earlier, skin-clad versions. The heads of three works in the exhibition were carved separately, in the manner of "stone head" dolls. There is a similar attention to the details of costume as in the skin dolls, revealing the detailed knowledge that came from making the real thing for family members. It is possible that there was an ambivalent attitude toward carving by the men of this isolated community because of this link with a woman's craft. They did not know that the men were doing the carving in the other communities to which Houston travelled regularly in those early years—an important consideation in a culture with clear sex-defined roles.[7]

KUUJJUARAAPIK

Kuujjuaraapik (formerly Great Whale River and Poste-de-la-Baleine), Nunavik's southernmost hamlet, is a bilingual community of Inuit and Cree. It was the site of a military base in World War II and a radar station was built there in 1955. The population of the community decreased significantly in 1985 when many families relocated to Umiujaq, fearing the results of the Great Whale River hydroelectric project.

As there has been employment from these various projects, few people have been involved in making carvings. But incentives, such as a co-operative that was formed in 1962 and a soft, finely-textured, dark green stone similar to that used in Sanikiluaq, may have encouraged the best-known artists, Henry Napartuk, Annie Niviaxie, and Lucy Meeko. Twomey collected 35 carvings by 17 known and 12 unknown artists including a stunning sculpture of a *Mother and Child* by Annie Niviaxie.

KANGIRSUK

The small community of Kangirsuk (formerly Payne Bay) has been home to a few well-known carvers over the years, particularly after a co-operative was established in 1964. Twomey collected seven sculptures from this community including one minor piece by the best-known artist from this community, Thomassie Kudluk. Two small treasures by lesser-known artists are included here.

IVUJIVIK

Ivujivik is a small community north of Puvirnituq that has not seen the development of many artists. Best-known in more recent years are the Iyaituk brothers, Nutaraaluk and Matiusi. Twomey collected 10 sculptures by 5 Ivujivik artists, including a carving by their father, Markusi, included here. Two other imaginative pieces by lesser-known artists are also included. ∎

5. Ibid., 16.

6. Graburn, 1969.

7. Wight, 1990.

BIBLIOGRAPHY – NUNAVIK

GENERAL

Fox, Matthew, Marybelle Mitchell and Grant Parcher. "Six Carvers from the East Coast of Hudson Bay." *Inuit Art Quarterly* 13, no. 3 (Fall 1998): 39-46.

Hessel, Ingo. *Inuit Art: An Introduction.* Vancouver/Toronto: Douglas & McIntyre, 1998.

Inuit Art Quarterly. "In Retrospect: Early Inuit Reports on Co-op and Carving Activities in Nunavik." *Inuit Art Quarterly* 13, no. 3 (Fall 1998): 22-35.

Makivik Corporation/Société Makivik Website: www.makivik.org/eng/communities.

Mitchell, Marybelle. "Making Art in Nunavik: A Brief Historical Overview." *Inuit Art Quarterly* 13, no. 3 (Fall 1998): 4-17.

Saucier, Céline and Eugen Kedl. *Image Inuit du Nouveau-Québec.* Québec: Musée de la Civilisation and La Corporation des Éditions Fides, 1988.

Saucier, Céline. *Guardians of Memory: Sculpture-Women of Nunavik.* Québec: Les éditions de L'instant même, 1998.

Swinton, George. *Sculpture of the Eskimo.* Toronto: McClelland and Stewart, 1972.

Swinton, George. *Sculpture of the Inuit.* Revised edition. Toronto: McClelland and Stewart, 1992.

von Finckenstein, Maria, ed. *Celebrating Inuit Art: 1948-1970.* Hull: Canadian Museum of Civilization, 1999.

Wight, Darlene Coward. "The Handicrafts Experiment, 1949-53." In *The First Passionate Collector: The Ian Lindsay Collection of Inuit Art.* Winnipeg: The Winnipeg Art Gallery, 1990.

INUKJUAK

Blodgett, Jean. "Port Harrison/Inoucdjouac Sculpture" in The Winnipeg Art Gallery, *Port Harrison/Inoucdjouac.* Winnipeg: The Winnipeg Art Gallery, 1977, p. 25-33.

Houston, James. "Port Harrison, 1948" in The Winnipeg Art Gallery, *Port Harrison/Inoucdjouac.* Winnipeg: The Winnipeg Art Gallery, 1977, p. 7-11.

Kasadluak, Paulosie. "Nothing Marvelous." Translated by Ali Tulugak; edited by Marybelle Myers, in The Winnipeg Art Gallery, *Port Harrison/Inoucdjouac.* Winnipeg: The Winnipeg Art Gallery, 1977, p. 21-22.

Myers, Marybelle. "In the Wake of the Giant," in The Winnipeg Art Gallery, *Port Harrison/Inoucdjouac.* Winnipeg: The Winnipeg Art Gallery, 1977, p. 13-20.

Roberts, A. Barry. *The Inuit Artists of Inoucdjouac, P.Q.* Montréal: La Fédération des Co-opératives du Nouveau-Québec and Ottawa: Department of Indian and Northern Affairs, 1978.

PUVIRNITUQ

Adams, Amy. "Surrealism and Sulijuk: Fantastic Carvings of Povungnituk and European Surrealism." *Inuit Art Quarterly* 9, no. 4 (Winter 1994): 4-10.

Blodgett, Jean. "Povungnituk Sculpture," in The Winnipeg Art Gallery, *Povungnituk.* Winnipeg: The Winnipeg Art Gallery, 1977, p .27-41.

La Fédération des Co-opératives du Nouveau-Québec. *Davidialuk.* Montréal: La Fédération des Co-opératives du Nouveau-Québec, 1977.

Fleck, Rev. James, S.J. "Steinmann of the North." *MacLean's* (August 1969): 36-42.

Murdoch, Peter. "Fivecentsiapik: The Little Five Cents." *Inuit Art Quarterly* 9, no. 3 (Fall 1994): 51-57.

Myers, Marybelle. "People Who Know How to Dream." *North* 22, no. 2 (March-April 1974): 32-35.

Myers, Marybelle. "The People of Povungnituk, Independent Through a Common Effort," in The Winnipeg Art Gallery, *Povungnituk*. Winnipeg: The Winnipeg Art Gallery, 1977, p.7-18.

Myers, Marybelle, ed. *Joe Talirunili: A Grace Beyond the Reach of Art*. Montréal: La Fédération des Co-opératives du Nouveau-Québec, 1977.

Nungak, Zebedee, and Eugene Arima. *Inuit Stories: Povungnituk/Légendes Inuit: Povungnituk*. Hull: Canadian Museum of Civilization, 1988.

Saladin d'Anglure, Bernard. *La parole changée en pierre: Vie et oeuvre de Davidialuk Alasuaq, artiste Inuit du Québec arctique*. Québec: Gouvernement du Québec, 1978.

Swinton, George. *Eskimo Fantastic Art*. Winnipeg: Gallery 1.1.1, University of Manitoba, 1972.

Swinton, George. "The Povungnituk Paradox: Typically Untypical Art" in The Winnipeg Art Gallery, *Povungnituk*. Winnipeg: The Winnipeg Art Gallery, 1977, p.21-24.

SALLUIT

Art Gallery of Windsor. *Sugluk: Sculpture in Stone 1953-1959*. Windsor: Art Gallery of Windsor, 1992.

Graburn, Nelson. *Eskimos Without Igloos: Social and Economic Development in Sugluk*. Boston: Little, Brown and Company, 1969.

Roberts, Barry A. *The Inuit Artists of Sugluk, P.Q.* Montréal: La Fédération des Co-opératives du Nouveau-Québec and Ottawa: Department of Indian and Northern Affairs, 1977.

Wight, Darlene. "Female Artists Excel in Salluit Collection." *Tableau* 3, no. 2 (March/April 1990): 3.

Wight, Darlene. *Women and Art in Salluit: The Poetry of the Early Sculpture*. Brochure. Winnipeg: The Winnipeg Art Gallery, 1990.

INUKJUAK ᐃᓄᒃᔪᐊᖅ

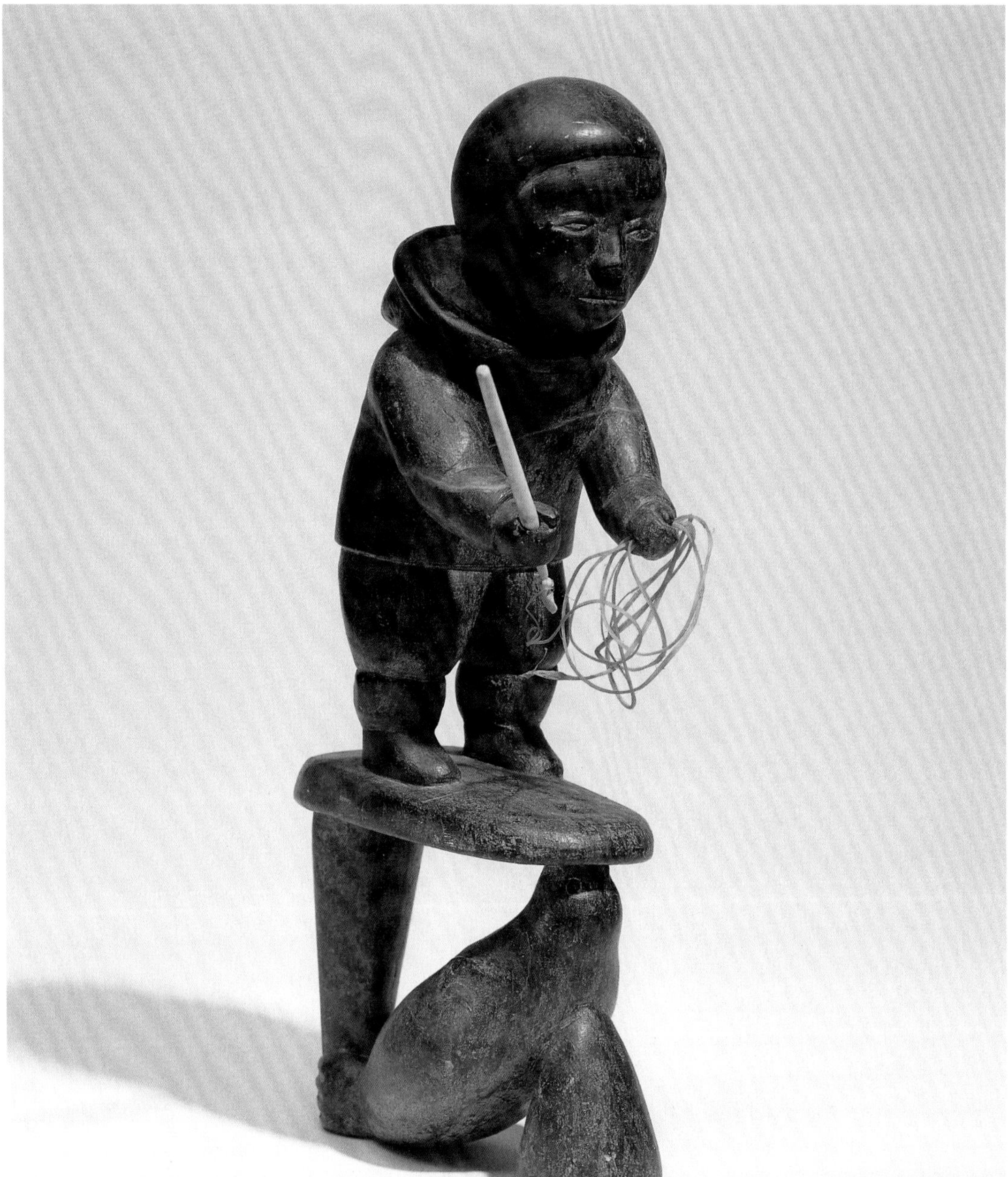

SAMWILLIE AMIDLAK, 1902-1984
ᓵᒧᐃᓕ ᐊᒥᓪᓚᒃ
Inukjuak ᐃᓄᒃᔪᐊᖅ
Hunter at Aglu
(Seal's Breathing Hole), 1967
stone, ivory, sinew
30.6 x 10.2 x 16.5
1816.71

ISA KASUDLUAK, 1917-1997
ᐊᓯ ᑲᓲᓗᐊᖅ
Inukjuak ᐃᓄᒃᔪᐊᖅ
Sculpin, 1963
stone
16.2 x 24.8 x 4.8
1876.71

JOSEPHIE ACULIAK, 1910-1968
ᔪᓯᕝ ᐊᖃᓕᐊᒃ
Inukjuak ᐃᓄᒃᔪᐊᖅ
Two Bears Fighting, 1962
stone
15.3 x 15.3 x 8.3
1843.71

TIMOTHY KUTCHAKA, b. 1924
ᑎᒧᑎ ᑯᑦᓴᒃ
Inukjuak ᐃᓄᒃᔪᐊᖅ
Man Inflating Avataq
(Sealskin Float), 1960-1961
stone
18.1 x 19.8 x 10.1
1770.71

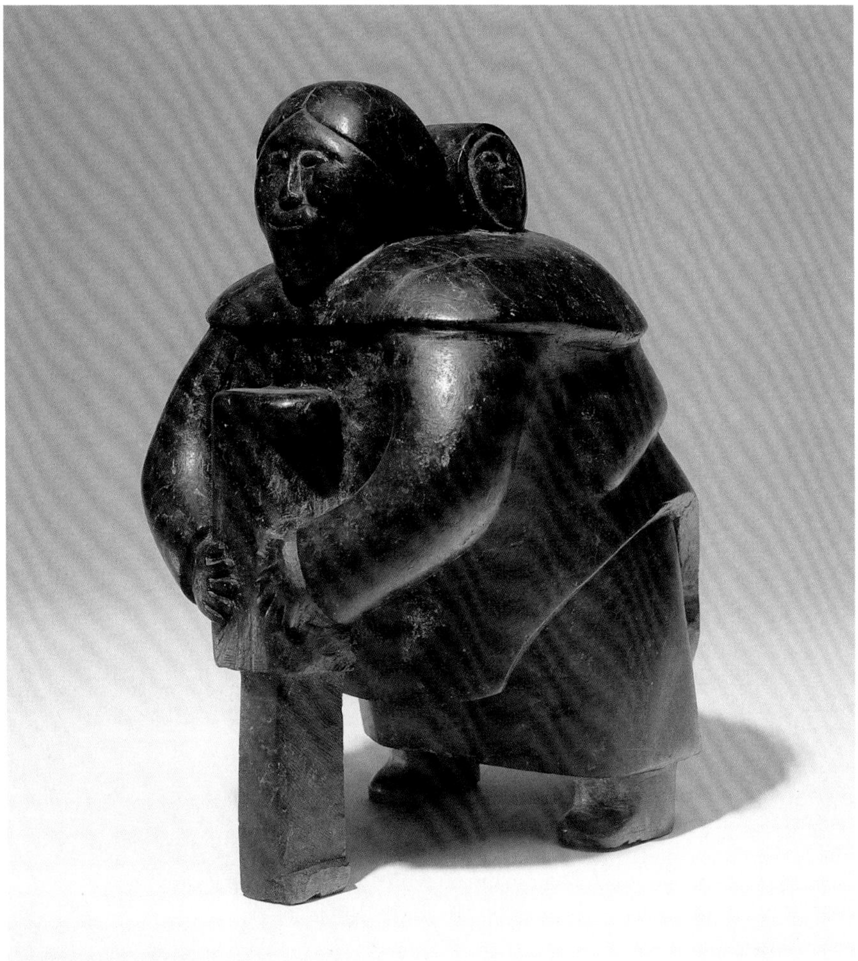

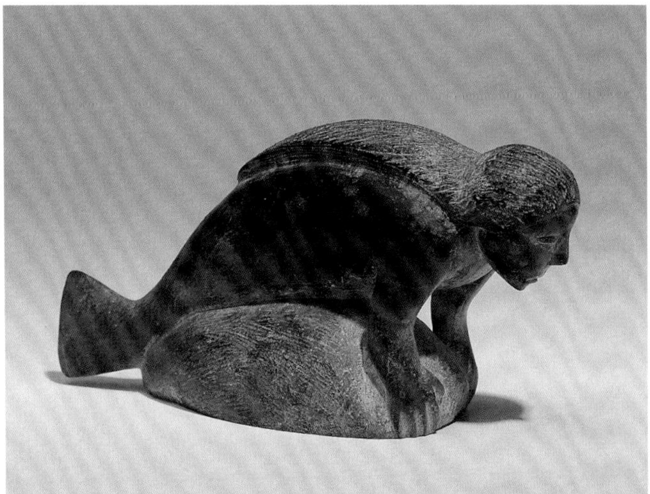

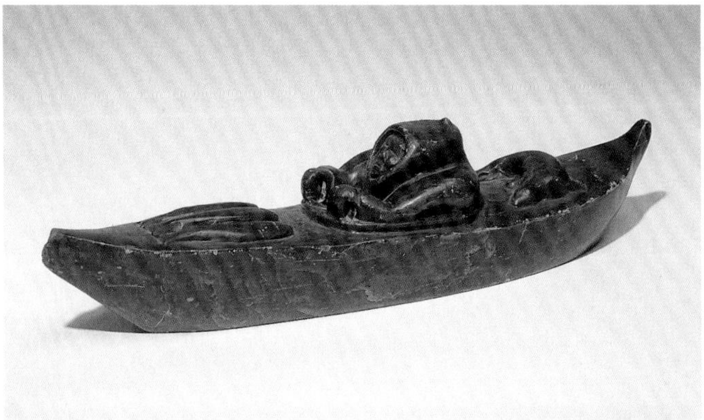

CONLUCY NAYOUMEALOOK
1940-1966
ᑯᓄᓘᓯ ᓇᔪᒥᐊᓗᒃ
Inukjuak ᐃᓄᒃᔪᐊᖅ
Woman Stretching and Shaping Kamik (Boot), c. 1962
stone
22.1 x 13.4 x 18.3
1826.71

SAMSON NASTAPOKA, b. 1931
ᓵᒻᓴᓐ ᓇᔅᑕᐳᑲ
Inukjuak ᐃᓄᒃᔪᐊᖅ
Sea Spirit, prior to 1971
stone
7.6 x 15.7 x 5
1889.71

LUCASSIE NOWRAKUDLUK
1912-1981
ᓘᑲᓯ ᓇᐅᕋᑯᑦᓗᒃ
Inukjuak ᐃᓄᒃᔪᐊᖅ
Man in Kayak, prior to 1971
stone
8 x 33.5 x 7.7
1856.71

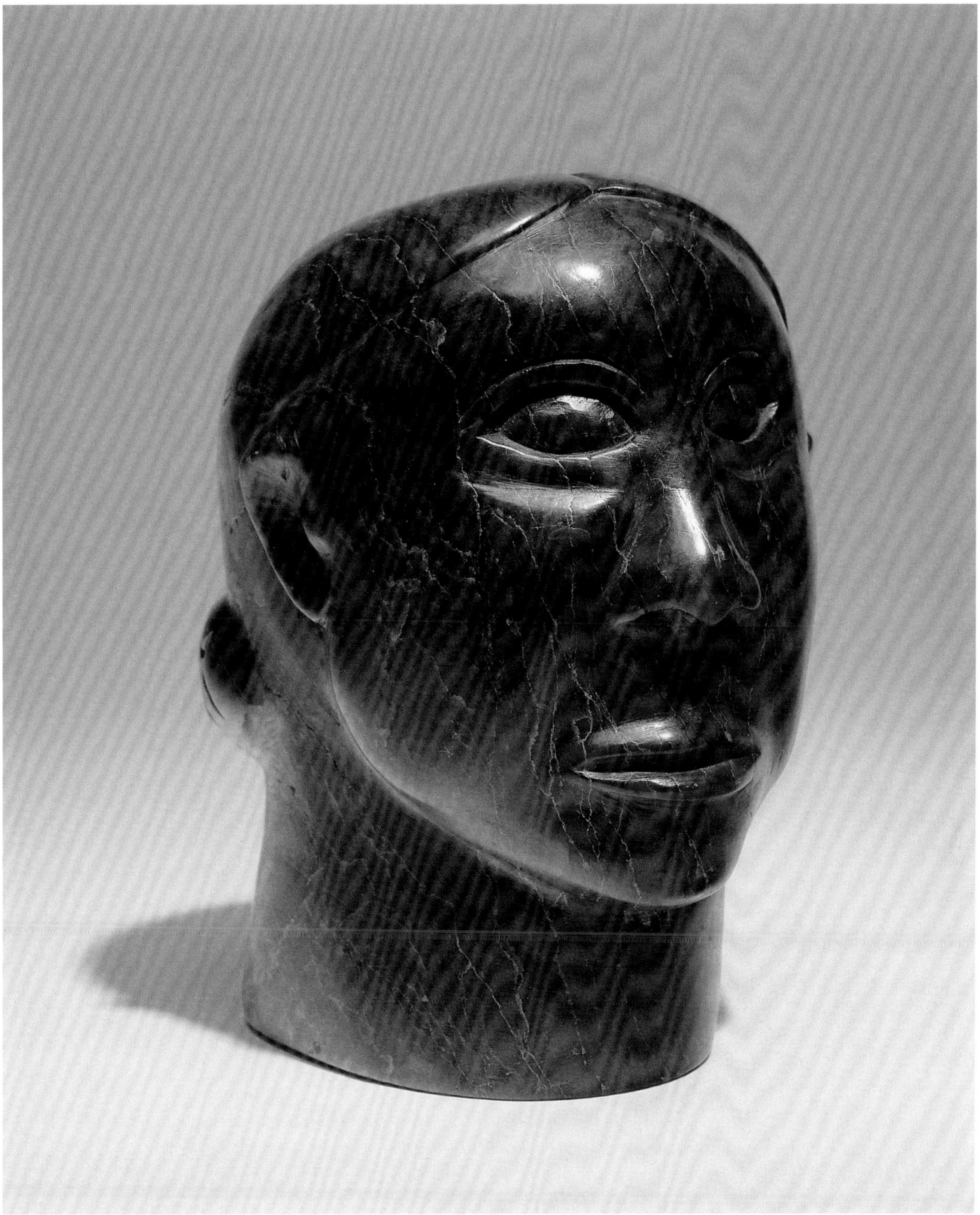

ABRAHAM NASTAPOKA
1900-1981
ᐄᐸᕋᒻ ᓇᔅᑕᐸᑲ
Inukjuak ᐃᓄᒃᔪᐊᖅ
Woman's Head, 1957
stone
15.1 x 10.7 x 13
1879.71

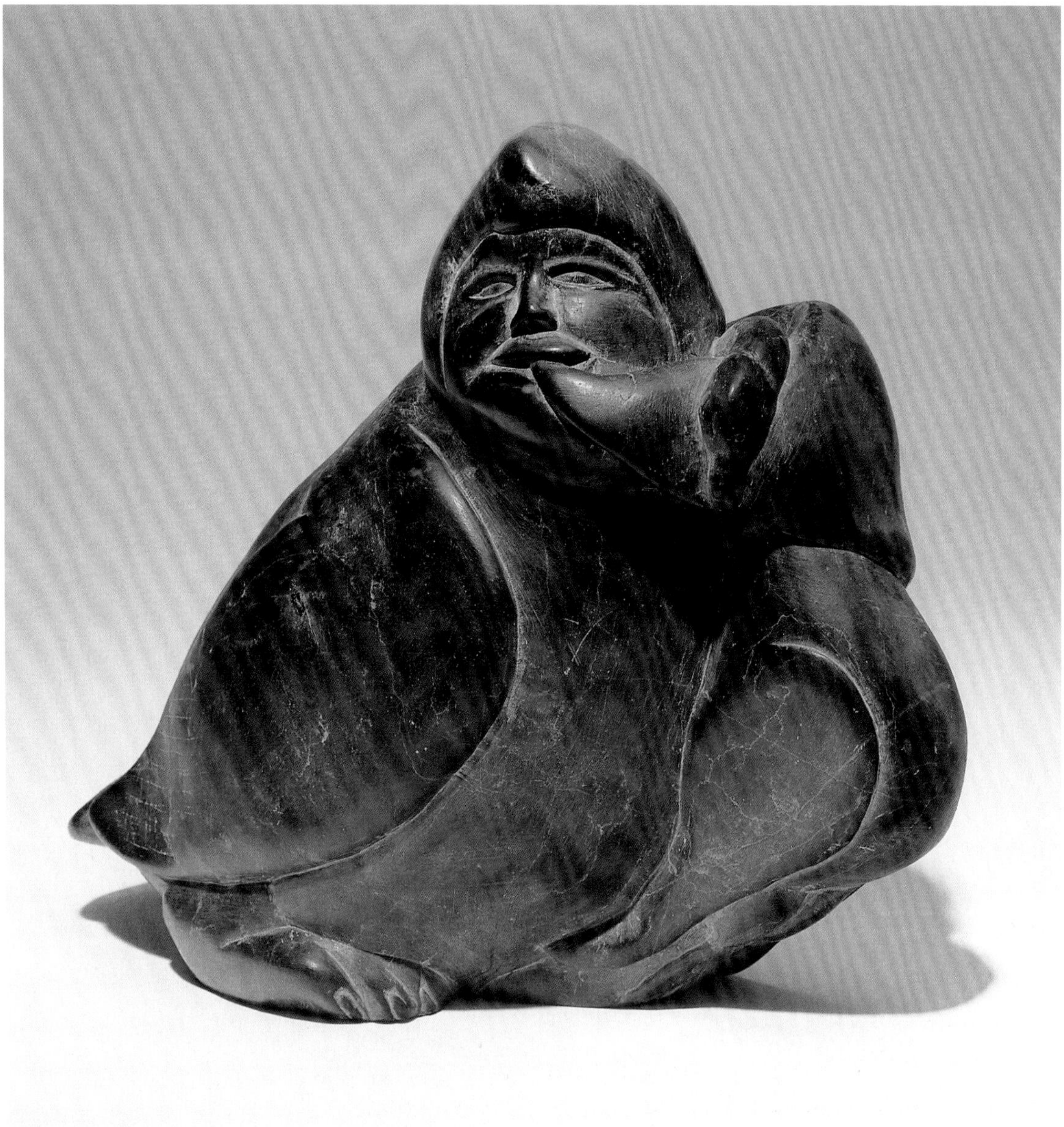

JOANASIE NOWKAWALK
b. 1926
ᔪᐊᓇᓯ ᓇᐅᑲᓪᓚᒃ
Inukjuak ᐃᓄᒃᔪᐊᖅ
Bird Shaman Holding Goose, 1962
stone
19.1 x 22.1 x 10.7
1801.71

LUCASSIE NOWRAKUDLUK
1912-1981
ᒍᑉᕐ ᴖᐅᕐᕿᑐᐦᑦᑉ
Inukjuak ᐃᓄᒃᔪᐊᖅ
Man Holding Four Heads,
prior to 1971
stone
11.1 x 5.8 x 8.2
1868.71

KILLUPA QINGALI, b. 1934
ᑭᓪᓗᐸ ᕿᖓᖠ
Inukjuak ᐃᓄᒃᔪᐊᖅ
Mother Goose and Young,
1960
stone
10.4 x 11.3 x 4.7
1901.71

ABRAHAM NASTAPOKA
1900-1981
ᐄᐳᕌ ᓇᑦᑕᐳᑭ
Inukjuak ᐃᓄᒃᔪᐊᖅ
Man Skinning Fox,
prior to 1971
stone
14.2 x 6 x 17.8
1880.71

JOANASIE NOWKAWALK
b. 1926
ᕐᑖᓇᕐ ᓇᐅᑉᕐᑖᑉ
Inukjuak ᐃᓄᒃᔪᐊᖅ
Sea Spirit with Seal, 1960s?
stone
14.8 x 9.5 x 20.2
1802.71

PUVIRNITUQ ᐳᕕᕐᓂᑐᖅ

DAVIDIALUK ALASUA AMITTU
1910-1976
ᑕᐃᐱᐊᓗᒃ ᐊᓚᓱᐊ ᐊᒥᑐ
Puvirnituq ᐳᕕᕐᓂᑐᖅ
Swimming Dog with Packs,
c. 1960
stone
7.7 x 21 x 11.3
1956.71

DAVIDIALUK ALASUA AMITTU
1910-1976
ᑕᐃᐱᐊᓗᒃ ᐊᓚᓱᐊ ᐊᒥᑐ
Puvirnituq ᐳᕕᕐᓂᑐᖅ
Spider, prior to 1965
stone
3.2 x 8.5 x 6.7
1959.71

DAVIDIALUK ALASUA AMITTU
1910-1976
ᑕᐃᐄᐱᐊᓗᒃ ᐊᓚᓱᐊ ᐊᒥᑦᑐ
Puvirnituq ᐳᕕᕐᓂᑐᖅᑐᖅ
Mythological Bird, 1958
stone
43.4 x 38.2 x 16.5
1953.71

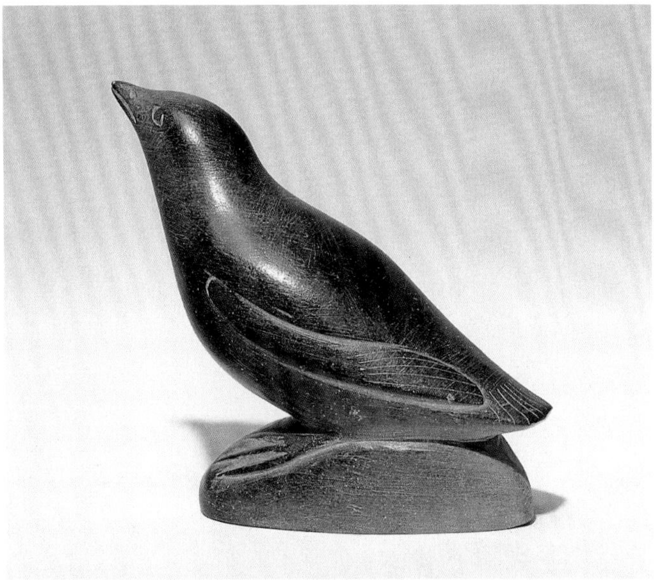

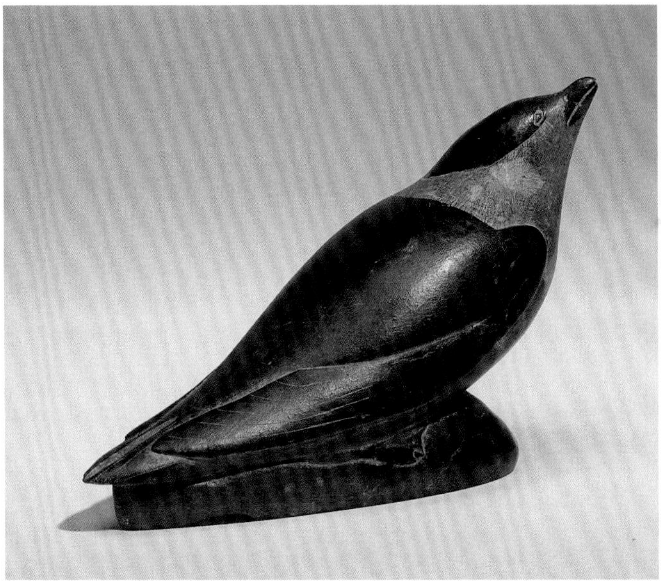

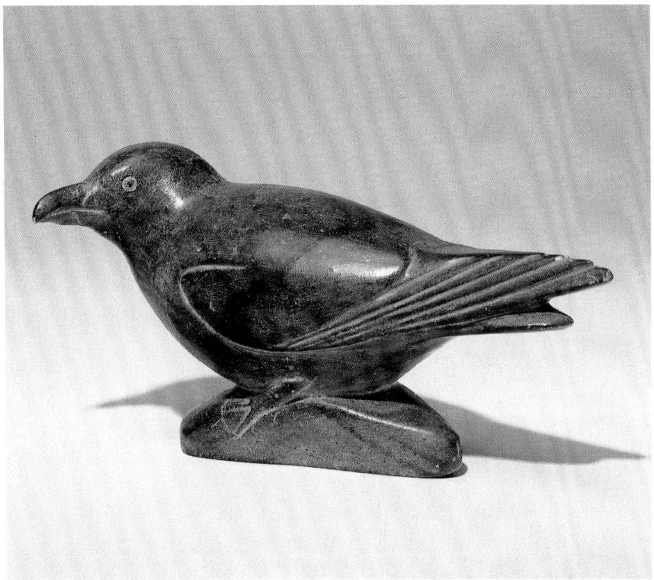

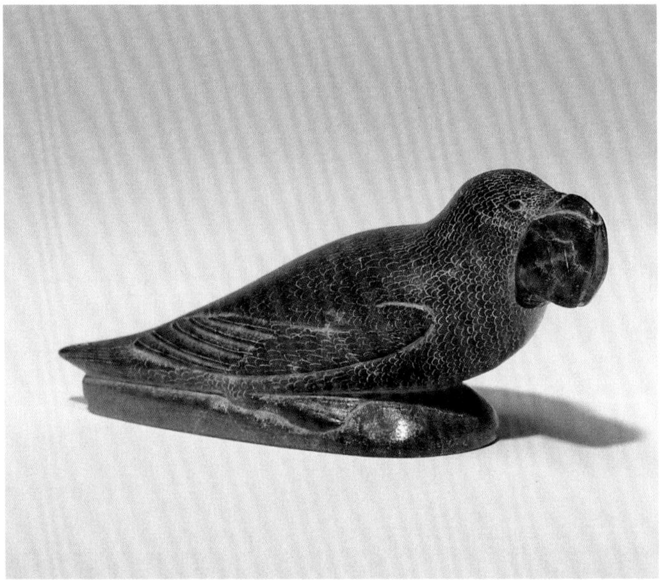

AISAPIK QUMA IGAUJA
1915-1979
ᐊᐃᓴᐱᒃ ᖁᒪ ᐃᒐᐅᔭ
Puvirnituq ᐳᕕᕐᓂᖅᑐᖅ
Dovekie?, c. 1961
stone
7.7 x 8.4 x 3.9
2029.71

AISAPIK QUMA IGAUJA
1915-1979
ᐊᐃᓴᐱᒃ ᖁᒪ ᐃᒐᐅᔭ
Puvirnituq ᐳᕕᕐᓂᖅᑐᖅ
Jaeger, c. 1961
stone
8.6 x 12.6 x 5.5
2020.71

SAMISA PASSAURALU IVILLA
b. 1924
ᓴᒥᓴ ᐸᔅᓴᐅᕋᓗ ᐃᕕᓚ
Puvirnituq ᐳᕕᕐᓂᖅᑐᖅ
Raven?, c. 1960
stone
7.9 x 15.4 x 6.9
1941.71

AISAPIK QUMA IGAUJA
1915-1979
ᐊᐃᓴᐱᒃ ᖁᒪ ᐃᒐᐅᔭ
Puvirnituq ᐳᕕᕐᓂᖅᑐᖅ
Gull, c. 1961
stone
5 x 12 x 3.9
2030.71

SAMISA PASSAURALU IVILLA
b. 1924
ᓴᒥᓴ ᐸᔅᓴᐅᕋᓗ ᐃᕕᓚ
Puvirnituq ᐳᕕᕐᓂᑐᖅ
Snow Goose, 1960
stone
13.2 x 16 x 6.8
1937.71

SAMISA PASSAURALU IVILLA
b. 1924
ᓴᒥᓴ ᐸᔅᓴᐅᕋᓗ ᐃᕕᓚ
Puvirnituq ᐳᕕᕐᓂᑐᖅ
Canada Goose, 1960
stone
11.5 x 16.6 x 6.6
1938.71

SAMISA PASSAURALU IVILLA
b. 1924
ᓴᒥᓴ ᐸᔅᓴᐅᕋᓗ ᐃᕕᓚ
Puvirnituq ᐳᕕᕐᓂᑐᖅ
Common Loon with Fish, 1960
stone
8.2 x 17.8 x 9
1939.71

SAMISA PASSAURALU IVILLA
b. 1924
ᓴᒥᓴ ᐸᔅᓴᐅᕋᓗ ᐃᕕᓚ
Puvirnituq ᐳᕕᕐᓂᑐᖅ
Snow Bunting?, c. 1960
stone
8.5 x 15.1 x 6
1940.71

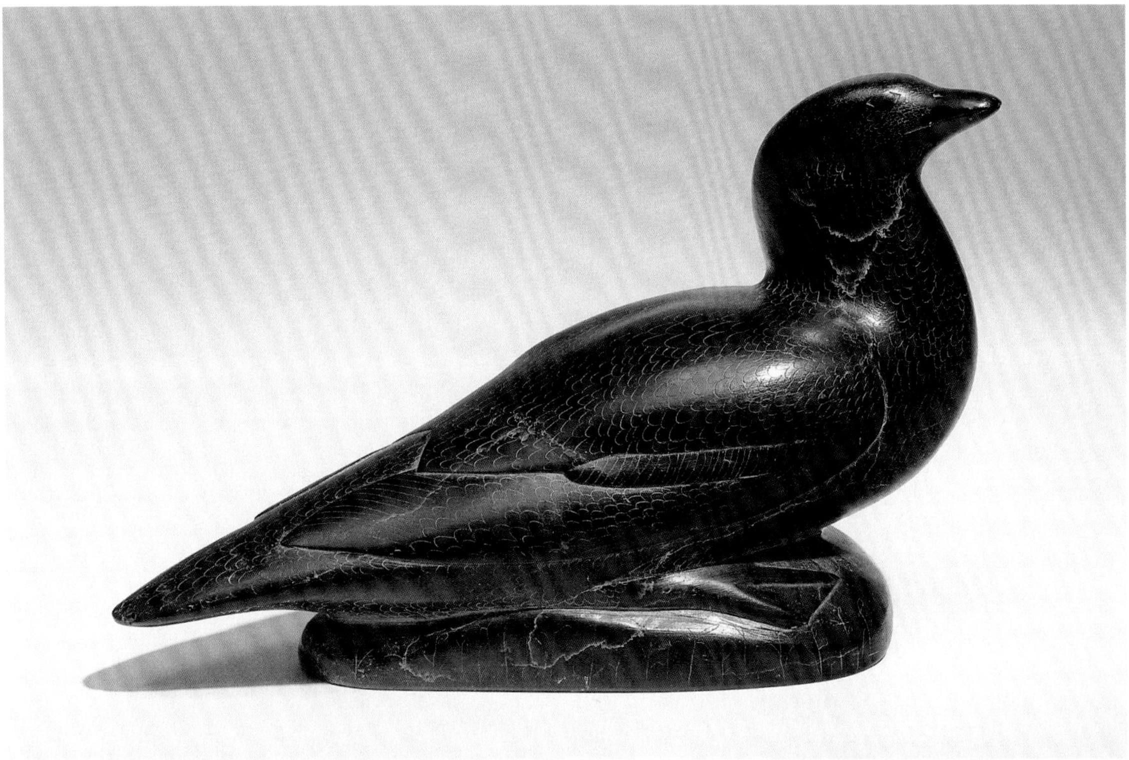

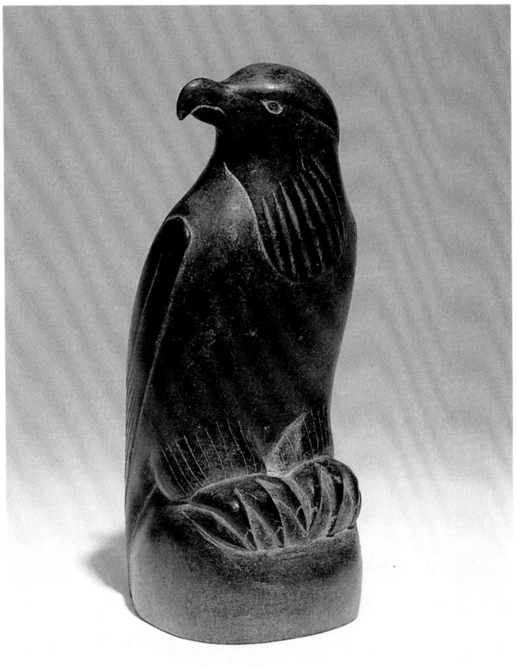

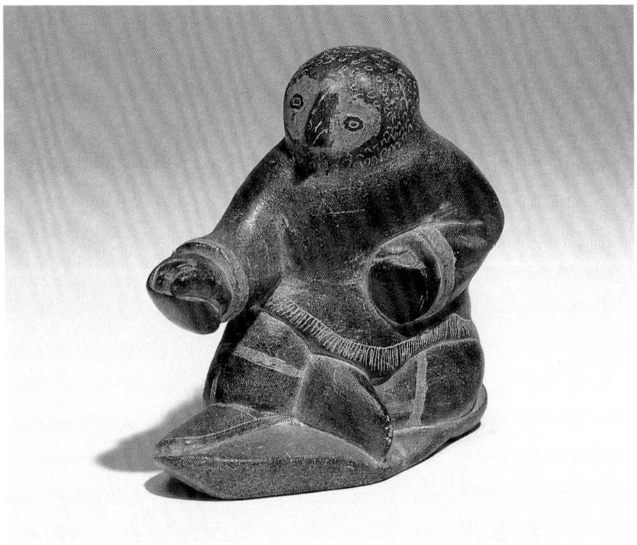

AISAPIK QUMA IGAUJA
1915-1979
ᐊᐃᓴᐱᒃ ᖁᒪ ᐃᒐᐅᔭ
Puvirnituq ᐳᕕᕐᓂᖅᑐᖅ
Duck, 1962
stone
10.2 x 16.3 x 6.8
2019.71

AISAPIK QUMA IGAUJA
1915-1979
ᐊᐃᓴᐱᒃ ᖁᒪ ᐃᒐᐅᔭ
Puvirnituq ᐳᕕᕐᓂᖅᑐᖅ
Gyrfalcon?, c. 1961
stone
21.4 x 10 x 9.6
2009.71

DAVID ALASUA TULLAUGU
b. 1941
ᑕᐃᕙᑦ ᐊᓚᓱᐊ ᑐᓪᓚᐅᒍ
Puvirnituq ᐳᕕᕐᓂᖅᑐᖅ
Owl Shaman Holding Lemming, 1961
stone
9.2 x 9.8 x 5.2
1981.71

ELI SALLUALU QINUAJUA
b. 1937
ᐃᓕ ᓴᓪᓗᐊᓗ ᕿᓄᐊᔪᐊ
Puvirnituq ᐳᕕᕐᓂᑐᖅ
Frog-like Spirit, prior to 1971
stone
27.3 x 28.3 x 11.1
1967.71

LEVI QUMALUK (attrib.),
1919-1997
ᓕᕓ ᖁᒪᓗᒃ
Puvirnituq ᐳᕕᕐᓂᑐᖅ
Man Skinning Duck, c. 1957
stone
12.6 x 11.1 x 15.2
1909.71

CONLUCY NIVIAXIE
1892-Unknown
ᑯᓄᔨ ᓂᕕᐊᒃᓯ
Puvirnituq ᐳᕕᕐᓂᑐᖅ
Mother Holding Baby,
prior to 1971
stone
16.5 x 13.9 x 13.4
1933.71

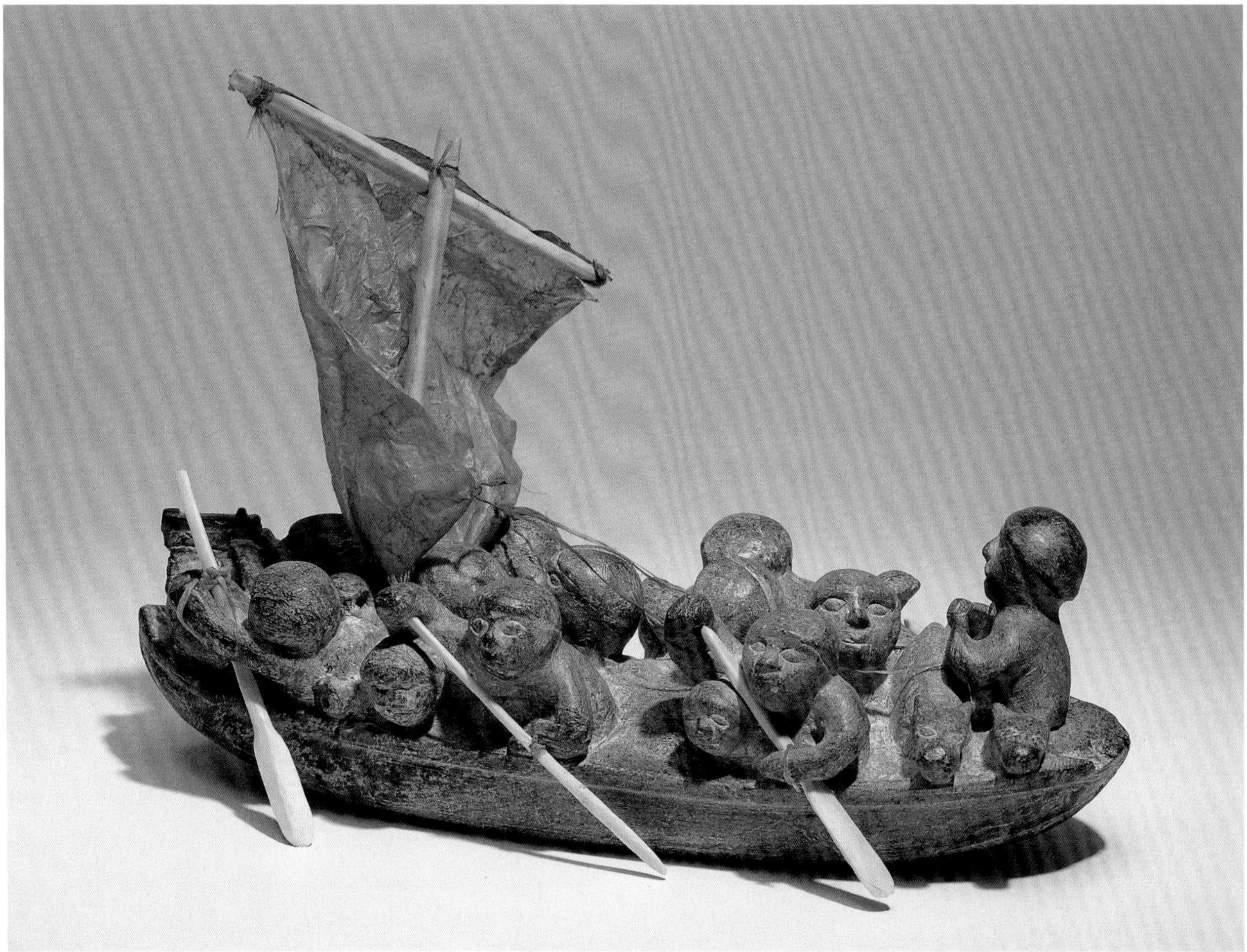

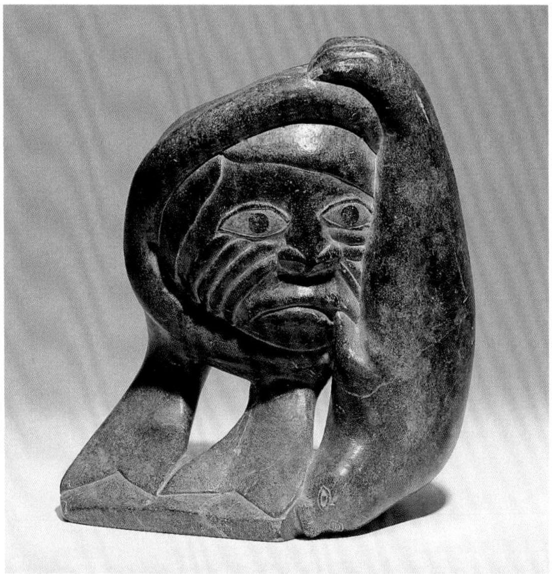

JOE TALIRUNILI, 1906-1976
ᔫ ᑕᓕᕈᓂᓕ
Puvirnituq ᐳᕕᕐᓂᕐᑐᖅ
Migration, c. 1965
stone, bone, gut, sinew
22 x 30.2 x 14.8
1951.71

JOHNIAHL JOHMAHL
ᔫᓂᐊᓪ ᔫᒪᓪ
Puvirnituq ᐳᕕᕐᓂᕐᑐᖅ
Legend of Man Who Ate Too Many Whales, c. 1962
stone
21.9 x 19.5 x 11.1
2034.71

JOE TALIRUNILI, 1906-1976
ᔪ ᑕᓕᕈᓂᓕ
Puvirnituq ᐳᕕᕐᓂᑐᖅ
Man Dragging Large Arm, 1959
stone
36 x 41.5 x 15.3
1950.71

SALLUIT ᓴᓪᓗᐃᑦ

MARY IRQIQUQ SORUSILUK
1897-1966
ᒣᐅᓇ ᐃᕐᕿᖅᑯᖅ ᓲᕈᓯᓗᖅ
Salluit ᓴᓪᓗᐃᑦ
Mother and Girl, c. 1957
stone
28.5 x 9.5 x 19.3
3960.71

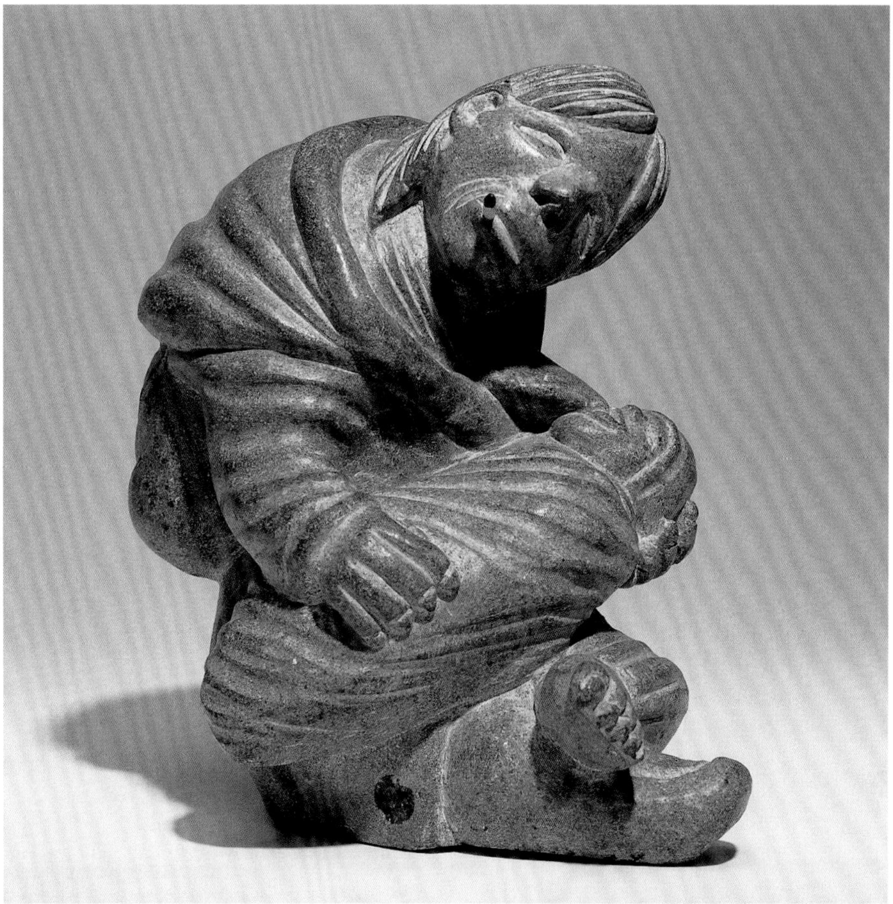

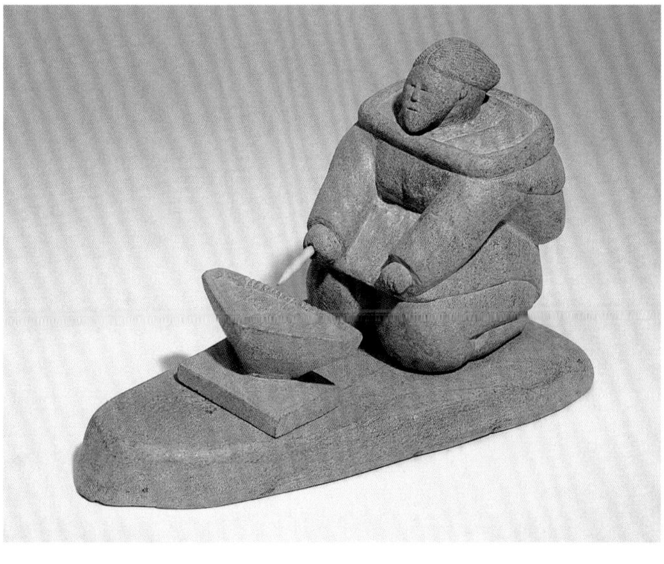

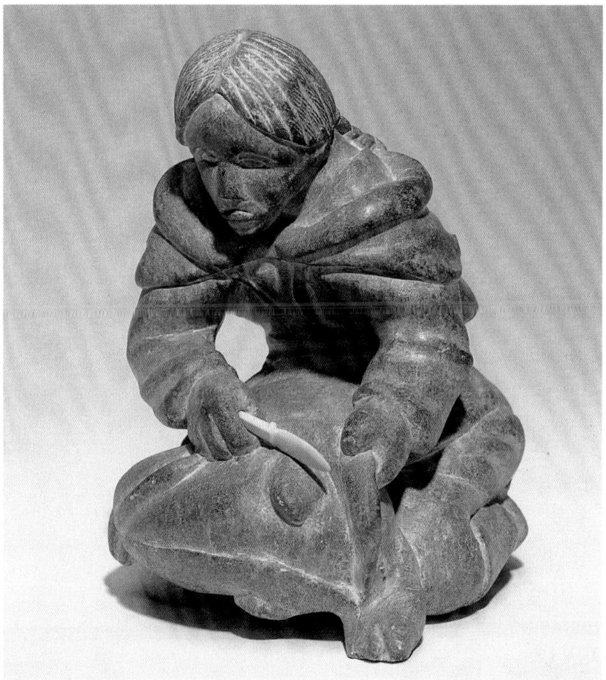

TIVI ILISITUK, b. 1933
ᑎᕕ ᐃᓕᓯᑦᑐᖅ
Salluit ᓴᓪᓗᐃᑦ
Smoking Mother Nursing Child,
c. 1957
stone, ivory
21.0 x 14.0 x 19.2
3985.71

MIAIJI UITANGI USAITAIJUK
(attrib), 1911-1965
ᒥᐊᔨ ᐅᐃᑕᖏ ᐅᓴᐃᑕᐃᔪᖅ
Salluit ᓴᓪᓗᐃᑦ
Woman with Qulliq (Stone Lamp), c. 1957
stone, ivory
14.7 x 12.1 x 23.6
3976.71

AUDLALUK KUPIRKRUALUK
b. 1926
ᐊᐅᓪᓚᓗᒃ ᑯᐱᕈᐊᓗᒃ
Salluit ᓴᓪᓗᐃᑦ
Woman Skinning Seal, c. 1961
stone, ivory
17.8 x 12 x 15.6
3953.71

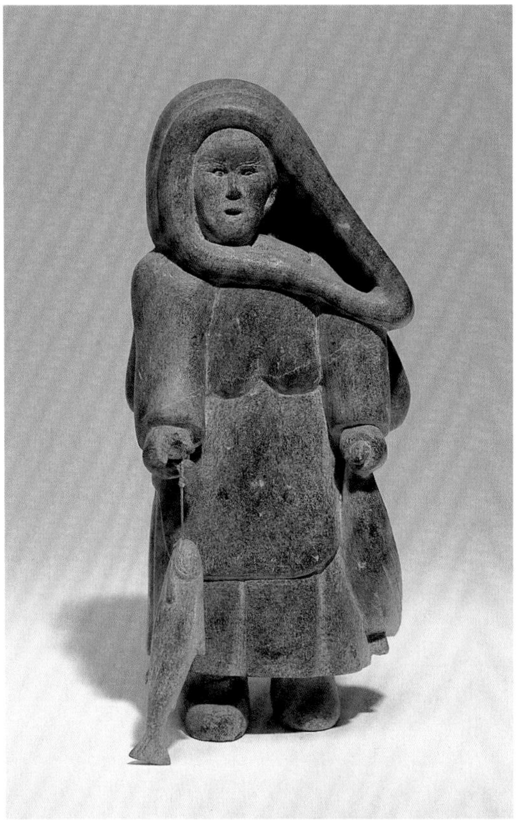

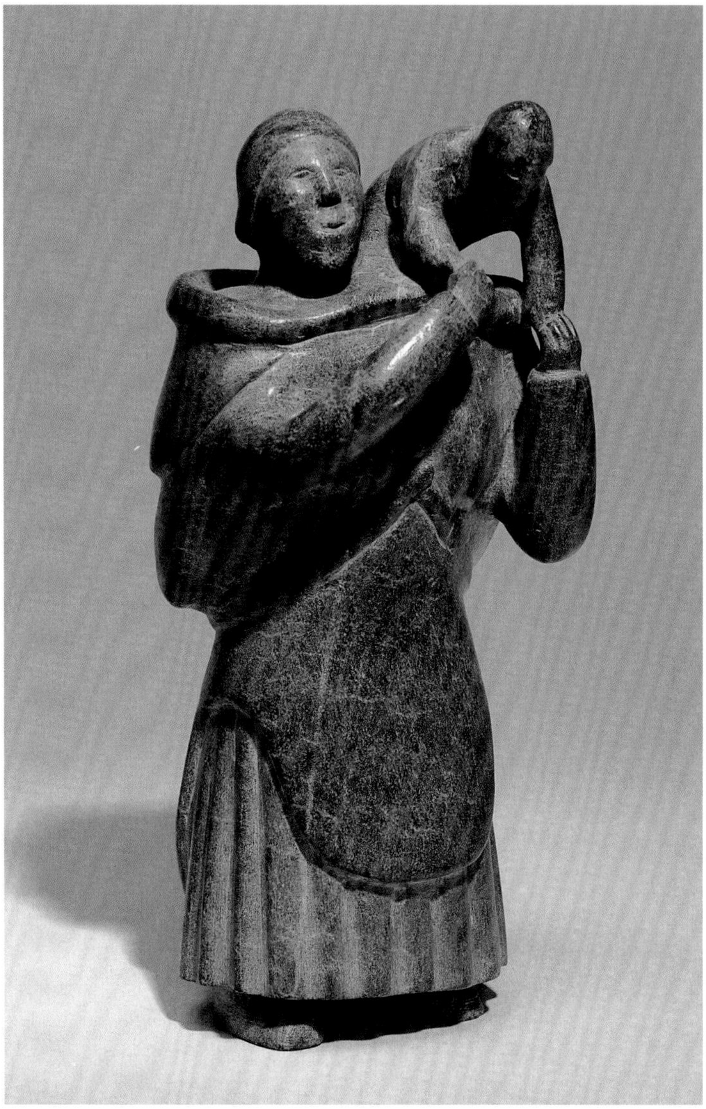

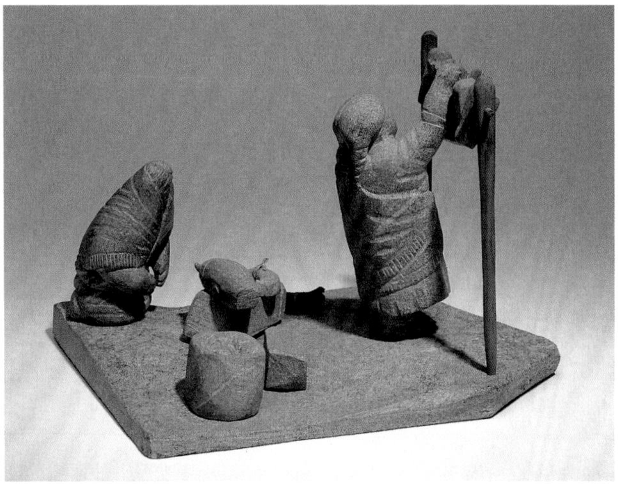

PIALLI TAYARAK, 1919-1964
ᐱᐊᓪᓕ ᑕᔭᕋᖅ
Salluit ᓴᓪᓗᐃᑦ
Woman Holding a Fish and a Goose, c. 1955
stone, wood, string
18.3 x 8.8 x 9.3
3950.71

MAGGIE ITTUVIK TAYARAK
1898-1961
ᒫᒋ ᐃᑦᑐᕕᒃ ᑕᔭᕋᖅ
Salluit ᓴᓪᓗᐃᑦ
Woman Removing Child from Amautik, c. 1961
stone
24.8 x 11.8 x 11.1
3973.71

UNKNOWN
ᐅᔨᒪᔭᐅᙱᑦᑐᖅ
Salluit ᓴᓪᓗᐃᑦ
Two Women Drying Meat, c. 1957
stone, wood, string
17.5 x 25.8 x 20
4004.71

KUUJJUARAAPIK ᑯᔪᐊᕋᐅᑉᐱᒃ

ANNIE NIVIAXIE, 1930-1989
ᐋᓂ ᓂᐅᐊᖅᓯ
Kuujjuaraapik ᑯᔪᐊᕋᐅᑉᐱᒃ
Mother and Two Children, 1966
stone
26 x 10.6 x 15.4
1627.71

SAMSON SALA, b. 1931
ᔅᒡᓴᐋ ᓴᓕ
Kuujjuaraapik ᖁᔾᔪᐊᕌᐱᒃ
*Shaman's Head with Bird
Spirits*, 1960s
stone
15.1 x 13.5 x 7.3
1630.71

ISSAC ALAYCO, b. 1941
ᐃᓴᒃ ᐊᓚᐃᑯ
Kuujjuaraapik ᖁᔾᔪᐊᕌᐱᒃ
Beaver, 1960s
stone, antler
9 x 7.5 x 7.8
1631.71

CHARLIE TUKTU, b. 1926
ᓵᓕ ᑐᒃᑐ
Kuujjuaraapik ᖁᔾᔪᐊᕌᐱᒃ
Successful Hunter with Bear,
1960s
stone
16.5 x 21.5 x 11
1618.71

DANIEL ANGUTIGULUK
1908-1980
Ċᴄᗞᐟ ᐊᵊᒍᑎᒍᒇᐟ
Kuujjuaraapik ᑯᕐᐸᐊᏑᐱ
Mother and Child, 1960s
stone
21.1 x 12.8 x 8.9
1613.71

LUCASSIE ALAYCO, b. 1942
ᒍᏴᕈ ᐊᴄᐃᑯ
Kuujjuaraapik ᑯᕐᐸᐊᏑᐱ
Woman Fishing, 1960s
stone, sinew
16.2 x 7.8 x 11.8
1624.71

KANGIRSUK ᑲᖕᒋᕐᓱᒃ

44

LUCASSIE LUCASSIE, b. 1911
ᓗᑲᓯ ᓗᑲᓯ
Kangirsuk ᑲᖕᒋᕐᓱᒃ
Woman Delousing Child, 1960s
stone
9.5 x 5.7 x 9.2
1727.71

JOSEPHIE EETOOK, b. 1913
ᔪᓯᐱ ᐃᑐᖅ
Kangirsuk ᑲᖕᒋᕐᓱᒃ
*Man Holding Child Above
Walrus*, 1960s
stone, ivory
20 x 11.4 x 8.3
1726.71

PAULUSI QAUNNAALUK
b. 1927
ᐸᐅᓗᓯ ᖃᐅᓐᓇᓗᒃ
Ivujivik ᐃᐳᕆᔨᒃ
Shamanic Journey, 1962
stone
13.9 x 15.8 x 6.5
1648.71

46

MARKUSI IYAITUK, b. 1906
Ĺdᒉ ᐃᐅᐊᑐᖅ
Ivujivik ᐃᐅᖨᐱᖅ
Birds on a Cliff, 1960s
bone, ivory, black colouring
13.5 x 17.5 x 14.2
2046.71

JUANISI NAUJA, 1927-1965
ᐊᖕᐅᓇᑦ ᐊᓇᐅᐅ
Ivujivik ᐃᐅᖨᐱᖅ
Whale Swimming Over Sculpin,
1960s
stone
6.0 x 13.3 x 8.6
1652.71

Qikiqtaalik Region

THE QIKIQTAALIK REGION IN THE TERRITORY OF NUNAVUT is also known as the Baffin region. It includes all of Baffin Island, as well as the communities of Igloolik and Hall Beach on Melville Peninsula, Grise Fiord on Ellesmere Island, and Sanikiluaq on the Belcher Islands in southeast Hudson Bay.

CAPE DORSET

After James Houston's visits to the Nunavik communities of Inukjuak and Puvirnituq in 1949-50, he turned his attention to Baffin Island. Visiting the Cape Dorset area in 1951, he was impressed by the stone carving being done. He encouraged carvers to create pieces for southern export. In 1954 an excellent carving stone was discovered at Aberdeen Bay within Markham Bay on the south Baffin Island coastline and this quarry is still a rich source of attractive stone. The colours of this serpentinite stone vary from jade green to green-black. The stone has a high degree of hardness and structural integrity, allowing considerable detail work and an almost virtuoso degree of piercing the stone. It retains its strength even when reduced to thin areas.[1] In 1959 a fishing co-operative was established in Cape Dorset and in 1961 this became the West Baffin Eskimo Co-operative, which has actively encouraged the creation of sculpture as well as graphic art to the present day.

Twomey first saw sculpture from Cape Dorset in the window of Robertson Galleries in Ottawa. He was very impressed and bought "about two dozen". While the Twomey Collection does not contain a large number of sculptures from Cape Dorset (166 sculptures by 63 known and 13 unknown artists), there are major works by many of the best-known carvers. The *Lion* by Kiawak Ashoona is one of the masterworks of the WAG Inuit Collection. There are a number of wonderfully bizarre "spirit" figures with transmuted bits and pieces of various animals that appealed to Twomey's sense of humour. Most are carved from the Aberdeen Bay green serpentinite.

ARCTIC BAY

Within the Twomey Collection there is a very special group of carvings from the small North Baffin community of Arctic Bay. It is probably the largest single

1. Gustavison, 1999, 45.

collection of work from that community—331 carvings by 56 known and 7 unknown artists, and it gives a very good sense of the carving activity that took place in the 1950s and 1960s. When the zinc mine at nearby Nanisivik opened in 1974, people gained employment in the mine and carving declined. Twomey was intrigued by the carvings that came from this remote community and he had asked to be notified whenever a box arrived from there, either at the Hudson's Bay Company or the Guild.

The stone used is a grey argillite, called *kooneak* locally, that is similar in appearance to the stone used in Sanikiluaq in southeast Hudson Bay, but with brownish blotches and streaks. Carvings are often made so the brown markings enhance their features. Since this hard stone occurs in thin layers, it is only possible to chop away relatively small pieces of stone. Thus the carvings are small and feature the intricate details that are easier to make in a hard stone without breakage.

In spite of the small scale of the works in the exhibition, there is an aura of consequence to the sculptures. Tiny details have been shaped with great care and fascinating subtleties reveal themselves to the patient observer. The animal carvings are alive with carefully observed and often enigmatic action— the rump of a diving bear visible behind the head of an unsuspecting walrus, two birds sitting on a human hand, a mother bird with a baby under each out-stretched wing, and the heads of two bears peering above the water. Carvings of people are often in motion and interacting as they carry on the actions of everyday life: a man teaching his son how to fish; two men resting in their travels, seated side-by-side on a *qamutiik*; a man cutting snow blocks; and a man struggling with a large box strapped to his back.

SANIKILUAQ

Sanikiluaq is located on the Belcher Islands in southeast Hudson Bay and although it is closer to the Nunavik region coast, it is part of the Territory of Nunavut. The Inuit residents of the islands called their land *Khikuktimee* ("the islands"), and called

themselves *Khikuktimiut*. The Inuktitut name, Sanikiluaq, refers to the legend of a famous hunter who could outrun a wolf or fox.[2] There were originally two Inuit camps on the north and south ends of Flaherty Island. In 1971 the federal government made the decision to centralize administrative operations in Sanikiluaq, the main settlement on the northern tip of the island.

Carving stone is readily available from a massive quarry on Tukarak Island 75 kilometres from Sanikiluaq.[3] Several smaller deposits are even closer. The stone is a grey-green or black argillite, similar in its finely grained texture to the grey-brown stone of Arctic Bay, and of neighbouring Kuujuaraapik on the mainland. As this soft, sedimentary stone fractures in layers, carvings are often small or thin in scale. Beginning in the early 1950s, carvings were purchased sporadically by the Hudson's Bay Company and the Great Whale River Co-operative. In 1968, the Metiq Co-operative was formed and this became an important buyer for carvers.[4] The style of sculpture from Sanikiluaq has always been realistic, and the stone, which can be polished to smooth, glossy surfaces, allows for meticulous details that are often incised into the stone with sharp tools.

In 1938 Jerry Twomey's ornithologist cousin, Arthur Twomey, made a scientific expedition to the Belcher Islands to conduct the first intensive study of the islands' bird life for the Carnegie Museum of Natural History in Pittsburgh.[5] Stories of Arthur's dogsled trip to the Belchers from Labrador intrigued Jerry, and he was interested in collecting carvings from the islands. There are 175 pieces by 43 known artists and 1 unknown artist in his collection. They date from 1960-1967 and include all the main artists of the period. Two works by hunting partners Johnny Meeko and Simeonie Uppik stand out for their originality. Uppik's *Man Inflating Avataq* is small yet powerful in its composition of balanced forms and repeated curves. The *Mother and Child* by Meeko is an individual statement of a classic theme as the bulky female form is firmly balanced on improbably slender legs. The Belcher Islands provide prime habitat for waterbirds, such as loons, geese, ducks, and gulls and these are common subjects for carvers.

1. Gustavison, 1999, 45.

2. See Driscoll in WAG, 1981, 37.

3. See essay by Patricia Sieber in WAG, 1981, 20-21.

4. Ibid., 19.

5. See Twomey and Herrick, *Needle to the North.*

The *Flock of Birds* by Lucassie Qittusuk is an exceptional example of this genre of work.

IQALUIT

Iqaluit (formerly Frobisher Bay) is now the capital of the Territory of Nunavut, but it did not exist until 1942 when the U.S. Air Force built an airport. Inuit from the surrounding area were hired to work on the construction. As there have been other opportunities for employment in Iqaluit, a carving industry was not as important as in the more remote communities. However, several Inuit have taken advantage of a local art market and have become distinguished artists. Although Twomey only collected nine sculptures from Iqaluit, they include strong pieces by well-known artists Ennutsiak, Noah Nuna, Henry Evaluardjuk, and Manno.

KIMMIRUT

Carvers from the small hamlet of Kimmirut (formerly Lake Harbour) now use the Aberdeen Bay stone as well, but in the 1930s and 1940s Kimmirut was a centre for ivory carving that was encouraged by the Hudson's Bay Company. Walrus tusks were imported from Igloolik and other areas for the carvers to fashion into intricate pieces such as finely detailed cribbage boards and engraved scrimshaw. Two fine contemporary examples of ivory carving from the Twomey Collection reveal that this tradition carried on into the 1960s in Kimmirut. The cribbage board is by Mosesie Kolola, a respected stone carver from the community.

Of the 48 Kimmirut pieces collected by Twomey, 26 are at least partially made of ivory. All stone pieces are from a light yellow or brownish-green serpentine. In a 1953 report, James Houston mentions "splendid stone deposits recently discovered," and that total output for the year would exceed $3,000.[6] By the 1970s, stone was the medium of choice by carvers from Kimmirut and the community has continued to be a centre for carving activity to this day.

PANGNIRTUNG

Pangnirtung was an important whaling area in the late 19th and early 20th centuries and skilled Inuit hunters were often employed by American and British whaling captains to man the whaling boats. Fat and the prized baleen were stripped from whales and taken away on ships by the visiting whalers. Bones were left behind, aging on the tundra. These ancient bones became carving material for Pangnirtung sculptors in the 1960s, as there was no nearby quarry of good carving stone.[7] There is little information available about the development of carving for export in Pangnirtung, but there are virtually no known whalebone carvings dating from the 1950s.[8]

Of the 21 pieces collected by Twomey from Pangnirtung, 18 are made from whalebone. Although dates are unknown for most of these carvings, they were probably made in the 1960s. Two of the most powerful whalebone pieces in the WAG Inuit Collection are by Pangnirtung artist Joanasee Kakkik, who has worked with the natural shapes of the vertebrae. ■

BIBLIOGRAPHY – QIKIQTAALUK

GENERAL

Driscoll, Bernadette. "Baffin Island Sculpture: The Winnipeg Art Gallery Collection." *Baffin Island*. Winnipeg: The Winnipeg Art Gallery, 1983, p. 33-45.

Gustavison, Susan. *Northern Rock: Contemporary Inuit Stone Sculpture*. Kleinberg: McMichael Canadian Art Collection, 1999.

Hessel, Ingo. *Inuit Art: An Introduction*. Vancouver/Toronto: Douglas & McIntyre, 1998.

Ryan, Terrence. "Art: An Evolution on Baffin Island." *Baffin Island*. Winnipeg: The Winnipeg Art Gallery, 1983, p. 27-31.

6. Wight, 1990, 77.

7. In a 1953 report by James Houston on carving activity in various communities, he notes that "splendid" skin sewing was being done as well as "some ivory work". There was no stone available and he suggested having it imported from Lake Harbour (see Wight, 1990, 77). See also Lister, 2002.

8. See Swinton, 1972.

Swinton, George. *Sculpture of the Eskimo*. Toronto: McClelland and Stewart, 1972.

Swinton, George. *Sculpture of the Inuit*. Toronto: McClelland and Stewart, 1992.

Wight, Darlene Coward. "The Handicrafts Experiment, 1949-53," in *The First Passionate Collector: The Ian Lindsay Collection of Inuit Art*. Winnipeg: The Winnipeg Art Gallery, 1990.

The Winnipeg Art Gallery. "Baffin Island: A Chronological History." *Baffin Island*. Winnipeg: The Winnipeg Art Gallery, 1983.

CAPE DORSET

Blodgett, Jean. "Osuitok Ipeelee," in *Inuit Art: An Anthology*. Winnipeg: Watson & Dyer Publishing, 1988.

The Winnipeg Art Gallery. *Cape Dorset*. Essays by James Houston, Alma Houston, Dorothy Eber, Terrence Ryan, Kananginak Pootoogook, Jean Blodgett. Winnipeg: The Winnipeg Art Gallery, 1980.

The Winnipeg Art Gallery. *Cape Dorset: Selected Sculpture from the Collections of The Winnipeg Art Gallery*. Winnipeg: The Winnipeg Art Gallery, 1975.

ARCTIC BAY

The Beaver. "Artists of Arctic Bay." (Autumn 1967): 20-25.

Cowan, Susan, ed. *We don't live in snow houses now: Reflections of Arctic Bay*. Ottawa: Canadian Arctic Producers, 1976.

Swinton, George. Review of *Ikpiarjuk: The Sculpture of Arctic Bay*. *Inuit Art Quarterly* 3, no. 3 (Summer 1988): 18-20.

Wight, Darlene. *Ikpiarjuk: The Sculpture of Arctic Bay*. Exhibition brochure. Winnipeg: The Winnipeg Art Gallery, 1987.

SANIKILUAQ

Hinds, Margery. "Mina." *The Beaver* 307 (Winter 1976): 20-24.

Kirwan, J. L. "Belcher Islands, N.W.T." *Canadian Geographical Journal* (September 1961): 84-89.

Twomey, Arthur C. "Walrus Off The Sleepers." *The Beaver* (December, 1938): 6-10

Twomey, Arthur C. and Nigel Herrick. *Needle to the North: The Story of an Expedition to Ungava and the Belcher Islands*. Boston: Houghton Mifflin Co., 1942.

The Winnipeg Art Gallery. *Belcher Islands/Sanikiluaq*. Essays by Bernadette Driscoll, Ed Horn, Patricia Sieber, and Dr. Spencer G. Sealy. Winnipeg: The Winnipeg Art Gallery, 1981.

KIMMIRUT

Driscoll, Bernadette. "Baffin Island Sculpture: The Winnipeg Art Gallery Collection." *Baffin Island*. Winnipeg: The Winnipeg Art Gallery, 1983, p. 33-45.

PANGNIRTUNG

Driscoll, Bernadette. "Baffin Island Sculpture: The Winnipeg Art Gallery Collection." *Baffin Island*. Winnipeg: The Winnipeg Art Gallery, 1983, p. 33-45.

Blodgett, Jean. "Whalebone," in *Inuit Art: An Anthology*. Winnipeg: Watson & Dyer Publishing, 1988.

Eber, Dorothy. *When the Whalers Were Up North: Inuit Memories from the Eastern Arctic*. Kingston, Montréal, London: McGill-Queen's University Press, 1989.

Harper, Ken. "Pangnirtung." *Inuktitut* (date unknown): 18-36.

Lister, Kenneth R. "The Inquisitive Dr. Bildfell." *Rotunda* (Summer/Fall 2002): 34-40.

CAPE DORSET ᑭᐊᕐᒥ ᐃᑦ

KIAWAK ASHOONA, b. 1933
ᑭᐊᕐᒃ ᐊᔨᓇ
Cape Dorset ᑭᐊᕐᒥ ᐃᑦ
Lion, 1960-1965
stone
23.9 x 23.5 x 26
1098.71

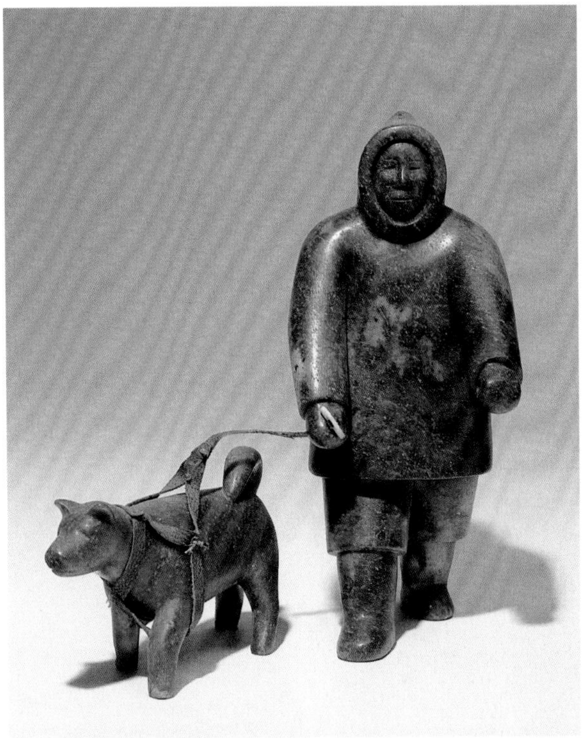

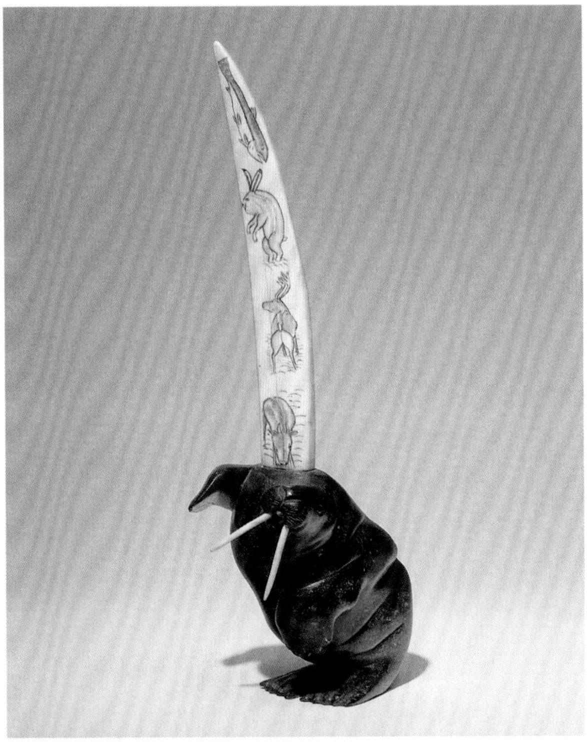

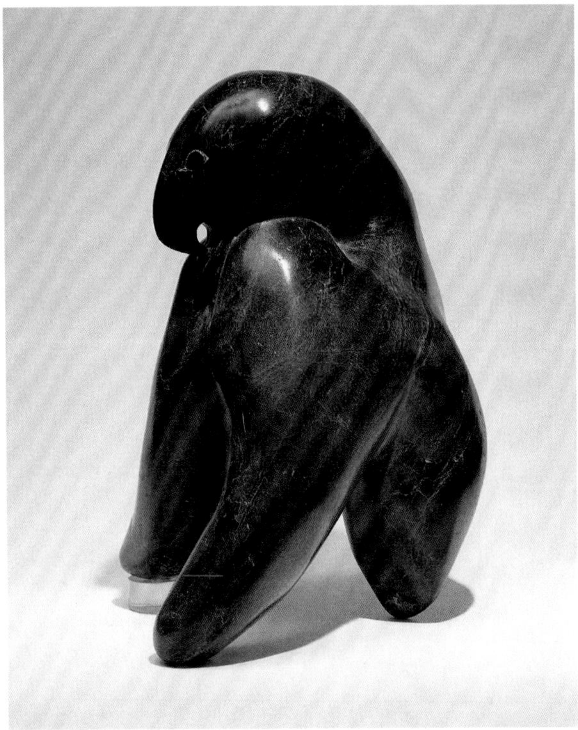

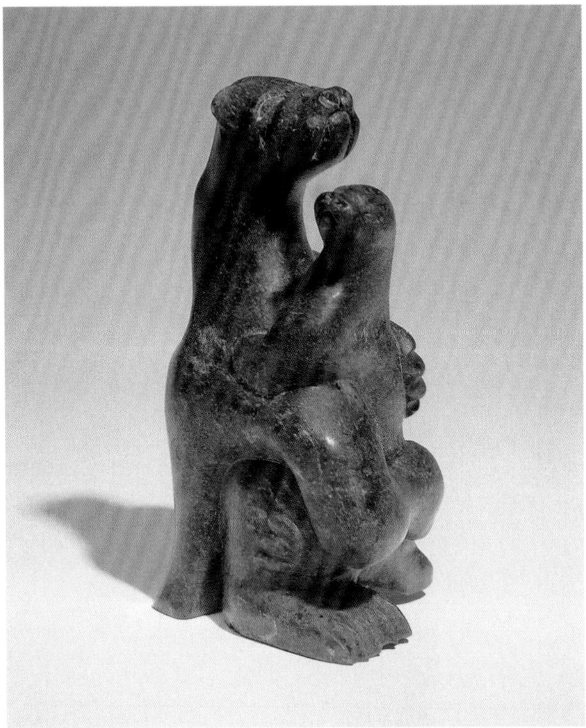

NIVIAKSIAK, 1908-1959
ᕕᐊᖅᓯᐊᖅ
Cape Dorset ᑭᙵᐃᑦ
Man with Harnessed Dog, 1956
stone, sealskin, antler
18.57 x 8.61 x 9.84
1087.71

KIAWAK ASHOONA, b. 1933
ᑭᐊᕚᒃ ᐋᓲᓇ
Cape Dorset ᑭᙵᐃᑦ
Walrus with Engraved Tusk, 1962
stone, ivory, crayon
36.6 x 9.3 x 14.1
1099.71

OSUITOK IPEELEE, b. 1923
ᐅᓱᐃᑦᑐᖅ ᐊᐃᐱᓕ
Cape Dorset ᑭᙵᐃᑦ
Hawk, 1965-1967
stone
45.8 x 25.9 x 33.3
1118.71

KIAWAK ASHOONA, b. 1933
ᑭᐊᕚᒃ ᐋᓲᓇ
Cape Dorset ᑭᙵᐃᑦ
Polar Bear Holding Seal, 1963
stone
17.1 x 12.9 x 9.5
1101.71

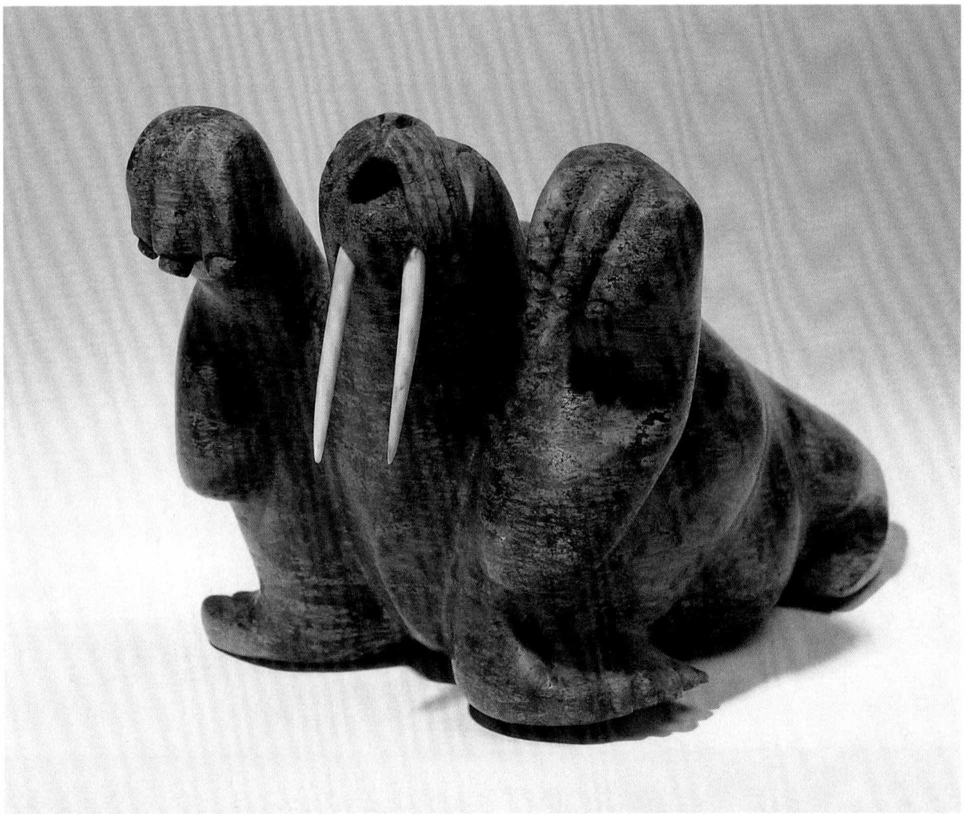

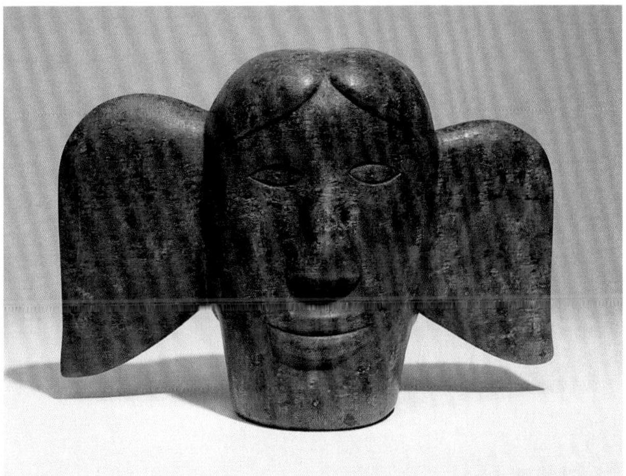

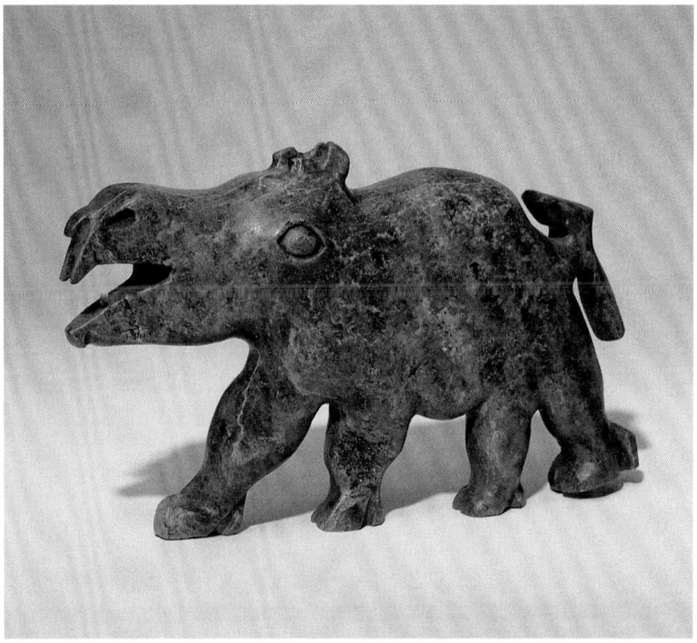

KAKA ASHOONA, 1928-1996
ᖃᖅᑲ ᐋᓲᓇ
Cape Dorset ᑭᓐᖓᓚᐃᑦ
Walrus Spirit, 1960-1965
stone, ivory
17.1 x 29.2 x 16.6
1092.71

JOANASSIE IGIU, 1923-1981
ᔫᐊᓇᓯ ᐃᒋᐅ
Cape Dorset ᑭᓐᖓᓚᐃᑦ
Winged Head, 1962
stone
18.7 x 26.8 x 13.3
1033.71

MIKIGAK KINGWATSIAK, b. 1943
ᒥᑭᒐᖅ ᑭᖑᐊᑦᓯᐊᖅ
Cape Dorset ᑭᓐᖓᓚᐃᑦ
Spirit, 1960-1965
stone
16.2 x 26.9 x 6.5
1020.71

54

KUMAKULUK SAGGIAK, b. 1944
ᑯᒪᑯᓗᒃ ᓴᒋᐊᒃ
Cape Dorset ᑭᙵᐃᑦ
Three-Headed Spirit,
1965-1967
stone
25.5 x 25.6 x 16.3
1132.71

KANANGINAK POOTOOGOOK
b. 1935
ᑲᓇᙵᓇᒃ ᐳᑐᒍᒃ
Cape Dorset ᑭᙵᐃᑦ
Owl, 1963
stone
14.3 x 14.5 x 8.2
1119.71

KUPPAPIK RAGEE, 1931-1995
ᑯᑉᐸᐱᒃ ᕋᒋ
Cape Dorset ᑭᙵᐃᑦ
Woman Holding Three Puppies,
1963
stone
25.4 x 16.5 x 21.2
1002.71

NINGEOSEAK PUDLAT, b. 1937
ᓂᙱᐅᓯᐊᒃ ᐳᓪᓚᑦ
Cape Dorset ᑭᙵᐃᑦ
Head of Dog, 1960-1965
stone
9.1 x 9.2 x 5.7
1008.71

AOUDLA PEE, 1920-2002
ᐊᐅᑦᓚ ᐱ
Cape Dorset ᑭᙵᐃᑦ
Bear's Head with Bear and Rabbit, 1965
stone, ivory
17.9 x 28.1 x 18.8
1071.71

EEGYVUDLUK POOTOOGOOK
1931-2001
ᐃᐱᐧᕝᓘᒃ ᑭᑐᒎᒃ
Cape Dorset ᑭᖕᖕᒥᐅᑦ
Bear Spirit, 1960-1965
stone
20.8 x 31.6 x 12.4
1140.71

PETER PITSEOLAK, 1902-1973
ᐲᑕ ᐱᓯᐅᓛᖅ
Cape Dorset ᑭᖕᖕᒥᐅᑦ
Engraved Walrus Tusk, c. 1965
ivory, stone, colouring
46 x 20.2 x 10.1
1030.71

EYEETSIAK PETER, b. 1937
ᐃᔨᑦᓯᐊᖅ ᐲᑕ
Cape Dorset ᑭᖕᖕᒥᐅᑦ
Bear and Raven Spirits
Fighting over Fish, 1963
stone
30.9 x 23.6 x 9
1117.71

AQJANGAJUK SHAA, b. 1937
ᐊᖅᖬᖬᒍᒃ ᖨ
Cape Dorset ᑭᖬᖬᒪᐃᑦ
Walrus, 1963
stone, ivory
23.9 x 36.3 x 14.2
1081.71

SIMIGAK SIMEONIE, b. 1939
ᓯᒥᒐᒃ ᓯᒥᐁᓂ
Cape Dorset ᑭᖬᖬᒪᐃᑦ
Spirit, 1960-1965
stone
13.7 x 28.6 x 17.9
1011.71

TUDLIK, 1890-1966
ᑐᑦᒃ
Cape Dorset ᑭᖬᖬᒪᐃᑦ
Double Owls, 1960
stone
10.8 x 10 x 7.2
1075.71

TOONOO, 1920-1969
ᑐᓄ
Cape Dorset ᑭᖕᖕᒥᐅᑦ
Mother and Child, 1960-1965
stone
16.5 x 6.9 x 7.7
1110.71

PAUTA SAILA, b. 1916
ᐸᐅᑕ ᓴᐃᓚ
Cape Dorset ᑭᖕᖕᒥᐅᑦ
Bear, 1962
stone
41 x 26.7 x 7.8
1042.71

ELISAPEE KANANGNAQ ALOOLOO
1918-1985
ᐃᒥᑲᐱ ᑲ_ᒧ_ᓴ ᐋᔅᔪ
Arctic Bay ᐃᑲᐱ◁ᔅᔪ
Female Bear Protecting Her Cub,
1960
whalebone, plastic
12 x 6.6 x 13.5
579.71

**ELISAPEE KANANGNAQ
ALOOLOO**, 1918-1985
ᐃᓕᓴᐱ ᑲᓇᖕᓇᖅ ᐋᓗᓗ
Arctic Bay ᐃᒃᐱᐊᕐᔪᒃ
Son Leading Father to Die,
1962
whalebone, baleen
16.6 x 13.2 x 5.1
320.71

**ELISAPEE KANANGNAQ
ALOOLOO**, 1918-1985
ᐃᓕᓴᐱ ᑲᓇᖕᓇᖅ ᐋᓗᓗ
Arctic Bay ᐃᒃᐱᐊᕐᔪᒃ
Mother and Child, 1962
whalebone
10.9 x 7.3 x 10.7
323.71

ATOAT AKITIRQ, b. 1935
ᐊᑐᐊᑦ ᐊᑭᑎᖅ
Arctic Bay ᐃᒃᐱᐊᕐᔪᒃ
Two Birds on Hand, 1966
stone
8.2 x 12.4 x 10.5
370.71

ATOAT AKITIRQ, b. 1935
ᐊᑐᐊᑦ ᐊᑭᑎᖅ
Arctic Bay ᐃᒃᐱᐊᕐᔪᒃ
*Man with Box Strapped to
Back*, 1966
stone, sealskin
9.6 x 12 x 12.5
369.71

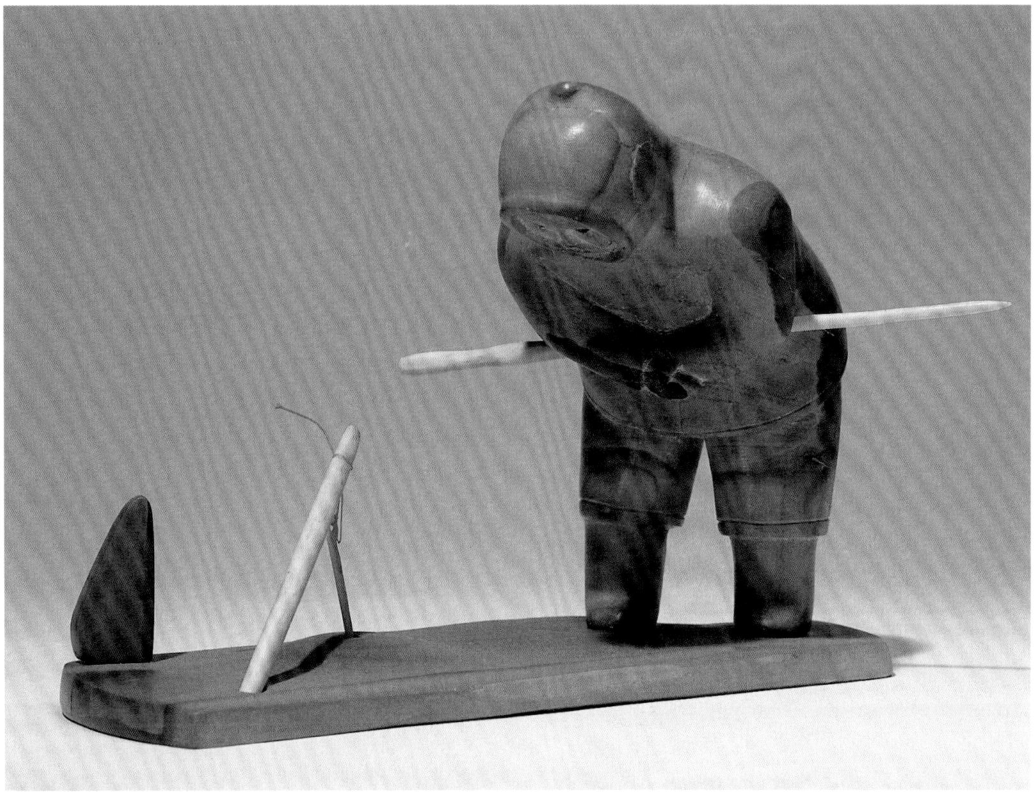

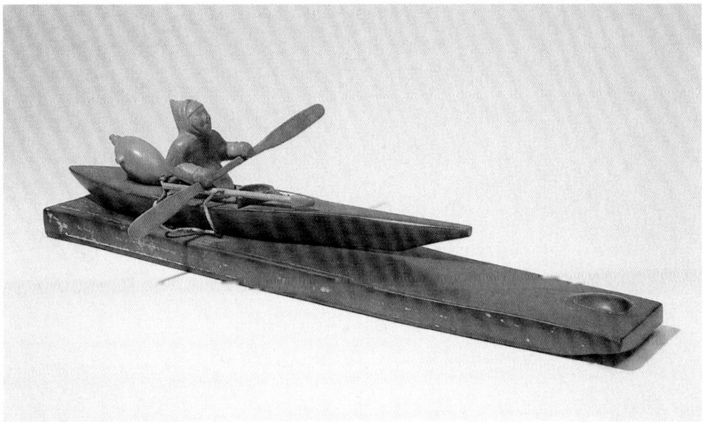

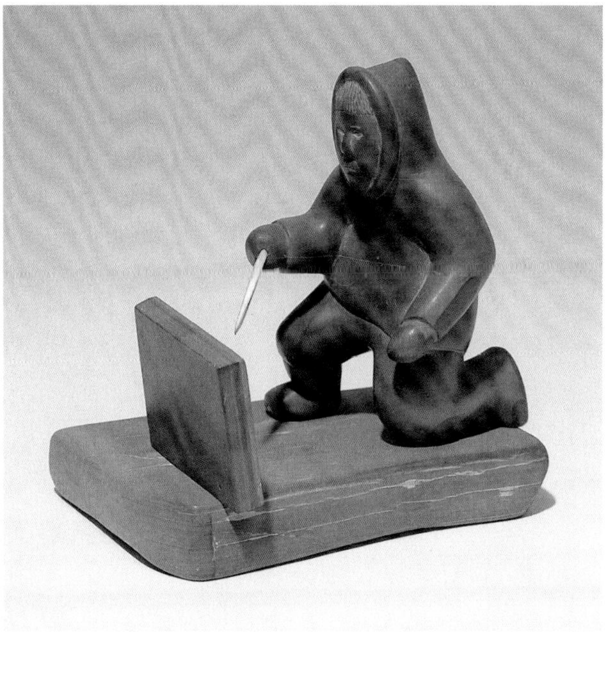

NAKYURAQ AKPALIAPIK
b. 1922
ᓇᒃᔪᕋᖅ ᐊᖅᐸᓕᐊᐱᒃ
Arctic Bay ᐃᒃᐱᐊᕐᔪᒃ
Hunter Waiting over Seal Hole,
1966
stone, antler, ivory, sinew,
baleen
12.4 x 19.4 x 11.4
550.71

PAULOOSIE AKITIRQ, b. 1935
ᐸᐅᓗᓯ ᐊᑭᖅᑎᖅ
Arctic Bay ᐃᒃᐱᐊᕐᔪᒃ
Hunter Paddling after Whale,
1966
stone, wood, hide, ivory
9.3 x 40.1 x 16.2
345.71

PAULOOSIE AKITIRQ, b. 1935
ᐸᐅᓗᓯ ᐊᑭᖅᑎᖅ
Arctic Bay ᐃᒃᐱᐊᕐᔪᒃ
Man Cutting Snow Block, 1966
stone, ivory
12.1 x 12.3 x 9.2
353.71

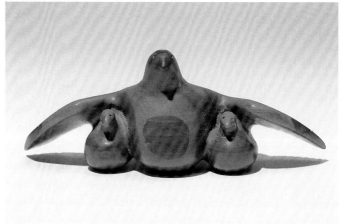

62

PHILIP QAMANIRQ, b. 1933
ᐱᓕᑉ ᖃᒪᓂᖅ
Arctic Bay ᐃᒃᐱᐊᕐᔪᒃ
Eider Duck, 1963-1966
stone
9.2 x 15.4 x 5.8
509.71

PETER ALOOLOO, 1908-1994
ᐲᑕ ᐊᔫᓗ
Arctic Bay ᐃᒃᐱᐊᕐᔪᒃ
Man with Fox, 1962
whalebone, ivory
14.4 x 12.3 x 5.1
301.71

PHILIP QAMANIRQ, b. 1933
ᐱᓕᑉ ᖃᒪᓂᖅ
Arctic Bay ᐃᒃᐱᐊᕐᔪᒃ
Ptarmigan and Young, 1964
stone
5.9 x 14.8 x 7.2
510.71

ZEBEDEE ENOOGOO, b. 1931
ᑭᐱᐣ ᐃᖢᒍ
Arctic Bay ᐃᑉᐱᐊᔅᔪᑉ
Man Carrying Seal, 1966
stone
14.3 x 9.7 x 6.7
420.71

PANILUK QAMANIRQ, b. 1935
ᐸᓄᒍᑉ ᖃᒪᓂᖅ
Arctic Bay ᐃᑉᐱᐊᔅᔪᑉ
Head of Bird/Shaman, c. 1965
stone
5.4 x 6.5 x 4.6
536.71

64

JOHN INERDJUK, b. 1938
ᐳᐊ ᐃᓂᕐᔪᒃ
Arctic Bay ᐃᒃᐱᐊᕐᔪᒃ
Heads of Two Bears, 1966
stone
4 x 10 x 4.5
294.71

DAVID ISSUQANGITUQ, b. 1937
ᑖᐁᑦ ᐃᓱᖃᖓᖕᑐᖅ
Arctic Bay ᐃᒃᐱᐊᕐᔪᒃ
*Construction with Knives and
Narwhal Tusk*, 1966
stone
16.7 x 18.8 x 5.5
260.71

AIBILLI KOONOO, b. 1940
ᐊᐃᐱᓕ ᑯᓄ
Arctic Bay ᐃᒃᐱᐊᕐᔪᒃ
Bear Diving After Walrus, 1965
stone, ivory
3.2 x 15.8 x 5.9
429.71

JOHN KOONOOK, b. 1939
ᐳᐊ ᑯᓄᒃ
Arctic Bay ᐃᒃᐱᐊᕐᔪᒃ
Husky Nursing Pup, 1961
stone, baleen
2.1 x 10.5 x 5.7
386.71

ATTAGOOTAK INNOTIK, b. 1929
ᐊᑕᒍᑦᑳᖅ   ᐃᓅᑎᖅ
Arctic Bay ᐃᒃᐱᐊᕐᔪᒃ
*Two Men Seated on Qamutiik
(Sled)*, 1966
stone, thread
10.1 x 18.5 x 6.7
435.71

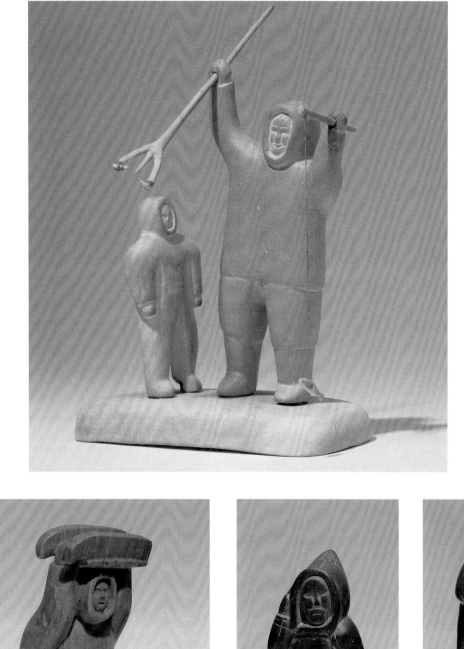

66

ATTAGOOTAK INNOTIK, b. 1929
ᐊᑕᒍᑦᕌᒃ ᐃᓅᑎᒃ
Arctic Bay ᐃᒃᐱᐊᕐᔪᒃ
Man Teaching Boy How To Fish,
c. 1966
stone, bone, thread
17.8 x 13 x 10.1
434.71

ATTAGOOTAK INNOTIK, b. 1929
ᐊᑕᒍᑦᕌᒃ ᐃᓅᑎᒃ
Arctic Bay ᐃᒃᐱᐊᕐᔪᒃ
Child Carrying Sled, 1965
stone
10.3 x 4.5 x 4.4
454.71

REBECCA ISSUGANGITUQ
b. 1936
ᕆᐸᒃ ᐃᓱᖕᒋᑦᑐᖅ
Arctic Bay ᐃᒃᐱᐊᕐᔪᒃ
Woman in Amautik, 1962
stone
11.9 x 4.7 x 3.5
265.71

REBECCA ISSUGANGITUQ
b. 1936
ᕆᐸᒃ ᐃᓱᖕᒋᑦᑐᖅ
Arctic Bay ᐃᒃᐱᐊᕐᔪᒃ
Woman Holding Fish, 1962
stone
13.5 x 4.8 x 4
264.71

SANIKILUAQ ᓴᓂᑭᓗᐊᖅ

JOHNNY MEEKO, b. 1933
ᔩᓂ ᒦᑯ
Sanikiluaq ᓴᓂᑭᓗᐊᖅ
Mother and Child, 1960s
stone
14.6 x 8.1 x 9.7
921.71

CHARLIE KUDLUROK, b. 1933
ᓯᑕ ᯅᶜᑐᑉᵇ
Sanikiluaq ᓴᓂᑭᓗᐊᑉᵇ
The Murder of a Dwarf, 1964
stone, wood, skin, ivory
16.6 x 14.7 x 10.9
991.71

SAMWILLIE IQALUQ, b. 1925
ᓯᯅᐃᑦ ᐃᑉᑊᑐᵇ
Sanikiluaq ᓴᓂᑭᓗᐊᑉᵇ
Sculpin, 1960s
stone
9.1 x 12.8 x 3.8
857.71

JOHNASSIE KAVIK, 1916-1984
ᯫᐊᑭ ᑲᯅᵇ
Sanikiluaq ᓴᓂᑭᓗᐊᑉᵇ
Woman Cooking, 1960s
stone
8.3 x 15 x 9.8
898.71

ISAAC AMITOOK, b. 1916
ᐊᐃᓴᒃ ᐊᒥᑑᖅ
Sanikiluaq ᓴᓂᑭᓗᐊᖅ
*Bear Standing on Bearded
Seal*, 1966
stone, ivory, wood
10 x 19.5 x 12.9
825.71

ALEC IPPAK, b. 1940
ᐋᓕᒃ ᐃᑉᐸᒃ
Sanikiluaq ᓴᓂᑭᓗᐊᖅ
Canada Goose in Flight, 1965
stone
13 x 41.7 x 24.5
883.71

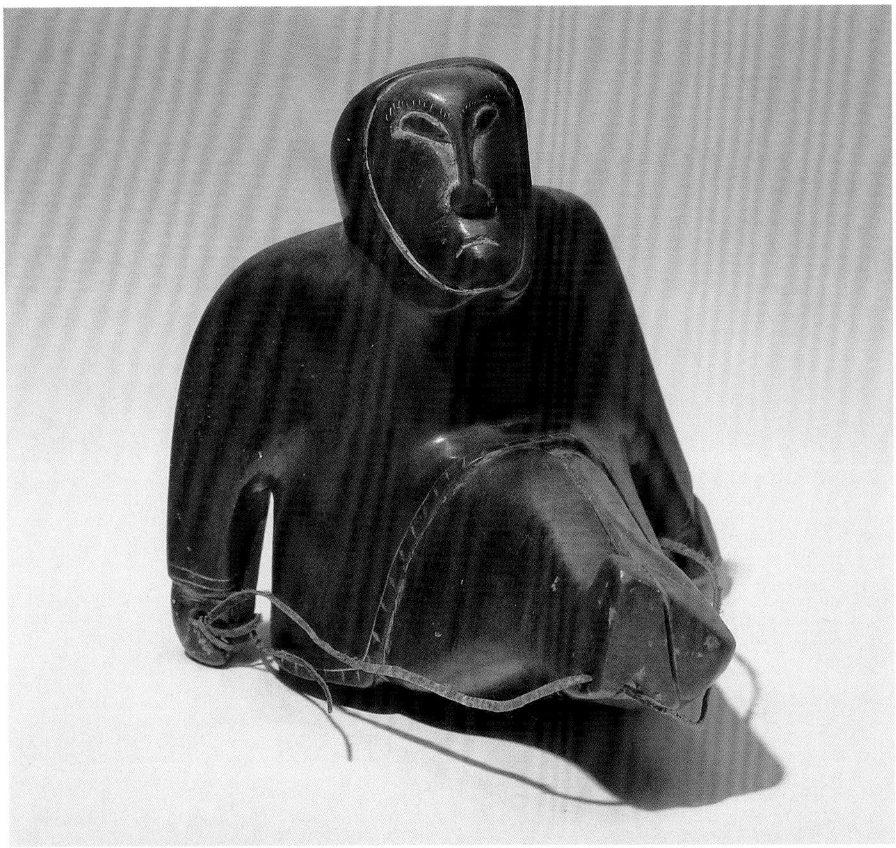

DAVIDEE KAVIK, b. 1915
ᑕᐃᕕᑎ ᑲᕕᒃ
Sanikiluaq ᑰᔾᔪᐊᕌᐱᒃ
Man Straightening Line, 1960s
stone, hide
10.7 x 10.4 x 11.4
1612.71

JOHNASSIE MANNUK, b. 1929
ᔪᐊᓇᓯ ᒪᓐᓄᒃ
Sanikiluaq ᓴᓂᑭᓗᐊᖅ
Man Spearing Seal, 1960s
stone, wood, sealskin
17.8 x 16.3 x 8.9
865.71

CHARLIE QITTUSUK, b. 1927
ᓵᓕ ᕿᑦᑐᓯᒃ
Sanikiluaq ᓴᓂᑭᓗᐊᖅ
Polar Bear, 1965
stone
8.5 x 23.2 x 5.5
956.71

SIMEONIE UPPIK, 1928-1988
ᔅᒥᐅᓂ ᐅᐸᕝ
Sanikiluaq ᓴᓂᑭᓗᐊᖅ
Man Inflating Avataq (Seal Skin Float), 1965
stone
22.1 x 4.8 x 11
927.71

SIMEONIE UPPIK, 1928-1988
ᒋᒥᐅᓂ ᐅᑉᐱᒃ
Sanikiluaq ᓴᓂᑭᓗᐊᖅ
Gull and Nest, prior to 1971
stone
11.5 x 15.2 x 5.3
928.71

JOHNASSIE TUKALLAK
1912-1988
ᔮᓇᓯ ᑐᑲᓪᓚᒃ
Sanikiluaq ᓴᓂᑭᓗᐊᖅ
Owl and Goose, 1960s
stone, wood
8 x 9.8 x 11.5
978.71

JOHNASSIE KAVIK, 1916-1984
ᔮᓇᓯ ᑲᕕᒃ
Sanikiluaq ᓴᓂᑭᓗᐊᖅ
Crawling Woman with Child,
1965
stone
8.8 x 13.1 x 17.4
892.71

LUCASSIE QITTUSUK
1908-1978
ᒍᑲᓯ ᖅᑐᒍᒃ
Sanikiluaq ᓴᓂᑭᓗᐊᖅ
Flock of Birds, 1960s
stone, wood
16.1 x 31.3 x 19
963.71

Iqaluit ᐃᖃᓗᐃᑦ

NOAH NUNA, b. 1900
ᓄᐊ ᓄᓇ
Iqaluit ᐃᖃᓗᐃᑦ
Mother and Children,
prior to 1971
stone
30.1 x 16.2 x 22.8
1594.71

ENNUTSIAK, 1896-1967
ᐃᓄᒡᓯᐊᖅ
Iqaluit ᐃᖃᓗᐃᑦ
Duck and Young, prior to 1971
whalebone, stone
23.5 x 34.9 x 23.5
1593.71

MANNO, 1923-1973
ᒪᓄ
Iqaluit ᐃᖃᓗᐃᑦ
Mother Duck and Ducklings,
prior to 1971
stone
9.2 x 9 x 18.7
1595.71

HENRY EVALUARDJUK, b. 1923
ᕼᐊᓐᓇ ᐃᕙᓗᐊᕐᔪᒃ
Iqaluit ᐃᖃᓗᐃᑦ
Polar Bear, prior to 1971
stone
24 x 18.8 x 11.9
1602.71

KIMMIRUT ᑭᒻᒥᕌᑦ

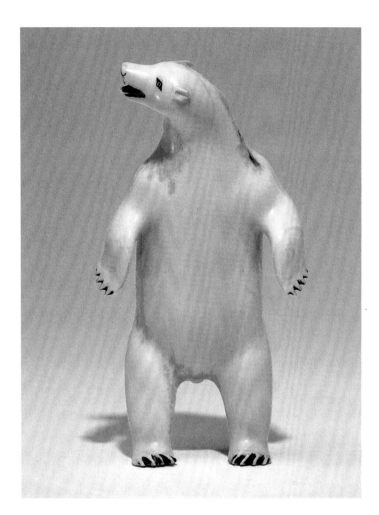

UNKNOWN
ᐅᖕᒥᔪᐊᖃᑦᑐᖅ
Kimmirut ᑭᒻᒥᕌᑦ
Polar Bear, 1955
ivory, black colouring, ink
11.4 x 6.3 x 5.4
1700.71

MOSESIE KOLOLA, 1930-1985
ᒧᓯᓯ ᑯᓗᓚ
Kimmirut ᑭᒻᒥᕌᑦ
Cribbage Board, c. 1960
ivory, stone, shoe polish, clay
7.3 x 44.2 x 9.5
1696.71

PANGNIRTUNG ᐸᖕᓂᖅᑐᖅ

JOANASEE KAKKIK
1919-1998
ᔪᐊᓇᓯ ᑲᒃᑭᒃ
Pangnirtung ᐸᖕᓂᖅᑐᖅ
Man and Woman, c. 1969
whalebone
35 x 66 x 22.1
1722.71

JOANASEE KAKKIK
1919-1998
ᐸᐃᐊᓯ ᑲᑭᒃ
Pangnirtung ᐸᖕᓂᖅᑐᖅ
Woman's Tattooed Face, 1970
whalebone, ivory
21.7 x 29.9 x 25.2
1720.71

Kivalliq Region

THE KIVALLIQ REGION IN THE TERRITORY OF NUNAVUT WAS formerly known as the Keewatin, and lies directly north of the Province of Manitoba. It is bordered on the west by the Northwest Territories and in the east it stretches along the coast of Hudson Bay. To the north it includes Coral Harbour on Southampton Island and Repulse Bay on Melville Peninsula.

BAKER LAKE

The community of Baker Lake has existed only since the 1950s and is inhabited by inland Caribou Inuit who had earlier lived in small, isolated family groups along the rivers—principally the Kazan, the Back, the Thelon, and the Prince—and beside the lakes—the Ennadai, the Yathkyed, the Maguse, and the larger Garry and Baker lakes. The people depended for food on the large caribou herds that migrated through the region in the fall of each year.

The 1950s was a period of disasters for inland Inuit groups in the Kivalliq region. A measles epidemic was followed by respiratory diseases including tuberculosis. In 1957 and 1958 there was poor fox hunting and the usual caribou herds were drastically reduced, causing starvation in hunting camps. Local government administrators encouraged people to move into Baker Lake where they could at least receive food and medical attention. An arts and crafts program was begun to give Inuit some means of self-sufficiency.

The first carvings for southern export began to appear in Baker Lake before Christmas in 1960.[1] The arrival of crafts development officer William Larmour, from the Department of Northern Affairs, in 1962 infused energy and expertise into the project and he made his small house into a crafts centre. Carvers such as Kingalik, Makpaaq, Sivuraq (Sevoga), Niuqtuq, Anguhadluq, and Amarook were the first to produce carvings, and others were soon to follow.[2] Since then, Baker Lake has become known for the powerful sculpture with round, bulging forms created from the hard, black and grey steatite stone found locally.

Jerry Twomey collected 244 carvings by 60 known and 29 unknown artists. The works all date from the 1960s, and include the square lines of a muskox by Luke Anguhadluq, the flowing curves of a *Kneeling Woman* by Francis Kaluraq, a *Caribou Scratching* by Vital Makpaaq, and an iconic *Mother and Children* by

1. The Winnipeg Art Gallery, 1964, 6.

2. Iglauer, 1964, 17-19.

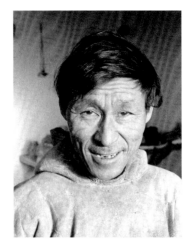

Arviat, February 1969. (Photo by Jerry Twomey)

Mark Alikasua, Arviat, February 1969. (Photo by Jerry Twomey)

Elizabeth Nutaraluk Aupaluktuk, Arviat, February 1969. (Photo by Jerry Twomey)

George Tatanniq. Women made carvings in the 1960s as well, and Martha Aptanik, Martha Tiktaq Anautalik, and Mary Singaqti Yuusipik are well-represented in the exhibition.

ARVIAT

The coastal region around present-day Arviat (formerly Eskimo Point) was originally home to the *Paallirmiut*, a group of Inuit who hunted sea mammals and sustained large hunting camps. They were later joined through government evacuations in the late 1950s by the inland *Ahiarmiut (Ihalmiut)*, and by ex-whalers from the Repulse Bay and Coral Harbour areas.[3] In an attempt to create income opportunities, soapstone was flown into the community in the winter of 1960/61.[4] Government arts and crafts officers began to arrive in Arviat on a temporary basis, and a craft shop and carving workshop were established in 1966. Artistic activity was considerable for 10 years.[5]

A distinctive minimalist style soon became evident. The carvers use the same type of hard, talc-rich steatite stones as those from Baker Lake.[6] The styles are sometimes more abstract, with less rounded forms. Surfaces are often left unpolished and the sculptures gain power from the hard, uneven textures of the raw stone. Much use has also been made of caribou antlers, which are shed annually.

Twomey collected a relatively large number of carvings (450) by Arviat artists in the late 1960s. About 170 of these are made of caribou antler instead of stone. Eighty-seven can be described as artifacts, or small-scale models of traditional weapons or tools. One hundred and eighty-seven of the identified pieces are by female carvers, a much higher proportion than in many other communities. The carvings by Margaret Aniksak Uyauperq and Lucy Tasseor Tutsweetok are stunning examples of their work at its very best.

Most of the Arviat subjects are human rather than animals, such as the tranquil *Mother Nursing Child* by Simon Katsuak and the unique antler work by Peter Komak showing only the heads of a mother packing a child in her amautik. An unusual sculpture in the oeuvre of George Arluk is a rugged shaman made of ancient whalebone. Forty-five pieces by John Pangnark were collected by Twomey, who considered his work "abstract art at its best. I got Pangnarks right at the beginning and bought every one I could get my hands on."[7] A black, polished *Seated Figure* is one of the artist's most accomplished carvings.

RANKIN INLET

In the 1950s the Canadian government established the communities of Arviat, Whale Cove, and Baker Lake along the west coast of Hudson Bay to facilitate the provision of food and supplies to Inuit who were expe-

80

3. Tagalik, 1998, 217

4. Kalluak, 1993, 5.

5. Hessel, 1990, 5.

6. See Gustavison, 1999, 85.

7. Twomey, taped interview in Winnipeg, September 24, 2002.

Madeleine Isserkut Kringayark, Nicolas Kringayark, and children Theresi, Paula, and Philippi, February 1969. (Photo by Jerry Twomey)

Louise Anguatsiark Tungilik, Mark Tungilik, and son Bernard. (Photo by Jerry Twomey)

riencing widespread starvation. But Rankin Inlet was formed with a different purpose. The settlement came into existence in 1955 when the mine began construction of its infrastructure, prompted by rising nickel prices during the Korean War. Inuit were brought in from all over the Kivalliq region to participate in this new experiment that introduced them to the skills and lifestyle of hard-rock mining. In 1957 the production of nickel concentrate began and for the next five years Rankin Inlet was a boom town. However, by 1960 it was realized that the ore body would not sustain long-term development, and the mine was closed in 1962. There was no plan for people suddenly without jobs, and the government encouraged people to move back to their areas of origin because it wanted to close the community. This was not an option welcomed by many residents and they negotiated with the government to fund the establishment of other employment projects, including the establishment of an arts and crafts project.

In April 1963 Claude Grenier, a fine arts graduate from Chicoutimi, Québec, was hired to organize this new project that had three main areas of concentration: sewing, carving, and the making of works in clay. Although there was a ready supply of carving stone from the tons of stone cleared from the mine, it was a very hard, porous stone and carvers were unable to create the fine details and polished surfaces that characterized stone carving in other communities.

But it was not long before a number of carvers had distinguishing themselves with a rugged aesthetic of simplified surfaces and primal subjects: mainly single human figures or mother-and-child groupings. John Tiktak and John Kavik are the best-known carvers from Rankin Inlet and both were collected by Twomey. Three fine works by Tiktak are featured in the exhibition. However, Twomey's collecting friend, George Swinton, was an avid follower of Tiktak's work and Twomey deferred to Swinton in the acquisition of the artist's work. In terms of abstraction, the artist closest to Twomey's heart was John Pangnark of Arviat.

REPULSE BAY

Repulse Bay is known by its inhabitants as *Naujaat* ("the place of gulls") and has been inhabited by *Arviligjuarmiut* since the 1600s. They have been carving for trade with visiting whalers since the late 19th century, and for export to the south since the 1940s, through the encouragement and marketing skills of Oblate missionaries in the community. Ivory miniatures were already a specialty in the region, and their small size kept the cost of shipping such items low. Although the use of ivory as a carving medium continues to this day, it has declined somewhat because of restrictions in the import of ivory into countries such as the U.S.

Felicite Kaunak, John Kaunak, and daughter
Beatrice, February 1969. (Photo by Jerry Twomey)

Alexania Nanordluk and Jaki Nanordluk,
February 1969. (Photo by Jerry Twomey)

Maria Mapsalak, February 1969.
(Photo by Jerry Twomey)

Mariano Aupillardjuk, February 1969.
(Photo by Jerry Twomey)

A local steatite stone was used increasingly in the 1960s. It came from Gore Bay, located about 60 miles from Repulse Bay. A mine was tunnelled 10 metres into a hill and stone was hand-quarried in October of each year. Carving was encouraged by Hudson's Bay Company post manager Henry Voisey when he lived in the community from the late 1950s to the mid-1960s.[8] The Naujat Co-operative was formed in 1968 and took over much of the purchase of carvings.

The collection of 1,669 Repulse Bay carvings assembled by Twomey is extraordinary for its size and breadth. As the pieces were small and relatively inexpensive, Twomey bought in bulk to indulge his geneticist curiosity. He believed that if he had a large enough sample of work, he might be able to determine if creativity was a hereditary characteristic that exhibited itself through strong familial connections. No definitive deductions were made, but this large sampling of carving is certainly a good overview of artistic activity in that community.

One interesting observation is that the medium of stone had become predominate in that period. Only 241 pieces included ivory, a notable shift from earlier times. It is also interesting that of the 95 known artists, 39 are women, a much higher proportion than in many other communities. The typically small scale of the pieces and relative softness of the grey or green Gore Bay steatite stone would have made carving possible for young or frail female carvers. Larger works are usually made up of several small figures pegged onto a base. This use of a carved base to give a physical context to the work is typical, and would have allowed complex pieces to be disassembled to minimize breakage when shipping.

Another key to collecting for Twomey was to have a large enough sample that the most talented carvers would be revealed. For Repulse Bay, one such talent emerged in the form of John Kaunak. Twomey pursued his work and collected an astonishing 88 carvings by the artist, dating from 1960 to 1969.[9] These are of a very high quality and a selection for the exhibition was difficult. From the four examples illustrated, it is possible to get a sense of the portrait-like realism of Kaunak's work, as in his *Whaling Boat*, that refers back to a genre of souvenir carving done for trade with whalers in an earlier era. His human figures and animals are always in energetic and realistically described motion. Faces have expressions that are occasionally so extreme they verge on caricature. Animals, such as his engaging polar bears, seem to come alive as they lumber pigeon-toed and snarl at unseen encounters.

Another well-known artist from Repulse Bay is Marc Tungilik, represented by 40 carvings in the Twomey Collection. His detailed ice fishing scene shows activity above and below the ice. ■

BIBLIOGRAPHY – KIVALLIQ

GENERAL

Gustavison, Susan. *Northern Rock: Contemporary Inuit Stone Sculpture*. Kleinberg: McMichael Canadian Art Collection, 1999.

Hessel, Ingo. *Inuit Art: An Introduction*. Vancouver/Toronto: Douglas & McIntyre, 1998.

Iglauer, Edith. "The Carvers of Keewatin." *Maclean's* (July 4, 1964): 42-43.

Marsh, Winifred Petchey. *People of the Willow: The Padlimiut Tribe of the Caribou Eskimo*. Toronto: Oxford University Press, 1976.

Mowat, Farley. *People of the Deer*. Toronto: University of Toronto Press, 1954.

Mowat, Farley. *The Desperate People*. Toronto: University of Toronto Press, 1959.

Oswalt, Wendell H. "Caribou Eskimo Without Caribou." *The Beaver* (Spring 1961): 12-17.

Soublière, Marion, ed. *The Nunavut Handbook*. Iqaluit: Nortext Multimedia Inc., 1998.

8. The Winnipeg Art Gallery, 1978, 27.

9. A date of 1963 has been given as the beginning of Kaunak's carving activities, but the dates of 1960 to 1962 are well-documented in the Twomey Collection. There are 14 pieces that date from 1960-62.

Swinton, George. *Sculpture of the Eskimo*. Toronto: McClelland and Stewart, 1972.

Swinton, George. *Sculpture of the Inuit*. Toronto: McClelland and Stewart, 1992.

Wight, Darlene. *The Swinton Collection of Inuit Art*. Winnipeg: The Winnipeg Art Gallery, 1987.

Williamson, Dr. Robert. "Spirit of the Keewatin." *The Beaver* (Summer 1965): 4-13.

The Winnipeg Art Gallery. *Eskimo Carvers of Keewatin N.W.T*. Essays by Ferdinand Eckhardt and W. T. Larmour. Winnipeg: The Winnipeg Art Gallery in co-operation with the Department of Transport and the Department of Northern Affairs and National Resources, 1964.

The Winnipeg Art Gallery. *The Zazelenchuk Collection of Eskimo Art*. Essays by Stanley Zazelenchuk and Jean Blodgett. Winnipeg: The Winnipeg Art Gallery, 1978.

Zepp, Norman. *Pure Vision: The Keewatin Spirit/Une vision pure: l'esprit du Keewatin*. Regina: Norman Mackenzie Art Gallery, 1986.

BAKER LAKE

Bouchard, Marie. *An Inuit Perspective: Baker Lake Sculpture from the Collection of the Art Gallery of Ontario, gift of Samuel and Esther Sarick*. Baker Lake: Itsarnittakarvik Inuit Heritage Centre, 2000.

Iglauer, Edith. "These magnificent carvings may keep these Eskimos in the stone age—where they like it." *Maclean's* (July 4, 1964): 17-19.

Keith, Darren. "Baker Lake." *The Nunavut Handbook*. Iqaluit: Nortext Multimedia Inc., 1998, 232-239.

ARVIAT

Canadian Arctic Producers. *Oonark/Pangnark*. Introduction by William E. Taylor, Jr. Ottawa: Canadian Arctic Producers, 1970.

Ducharme, Lionel, O.M.I. "History of Eskimo Point," in Comerford, E. and T. Suluk, eds. *Eskimo Point*. Altona: Friesen and Son Ltd., 1967.

Hessel, Ingo. "Arviat Stone Sculpture: Born of the Struggle with an Uncompromising Medium." *Inuit Art Quarterly* 5, no. 1 (Winter 1990): 4-10.

Inuktitut, no. 62 (Winter 1985): 2-30 (Several articles about Arviat).

Kalluak, Mark. *Pelts to Stone: A History of Arts and Crafts Production in Arviat*. Ottawa: Indian and Northern Affairs, Canada, 1993.

Swinton, George. "Artists from the Keewatin." *Canadian Art* no. 101 (April 1966): 32-34.

Tagalik, Shirley. "Arviat." *The Nunavut Handbook*. Iqaluit: Nortext Multimedia Inc., 1998, p. 217-223.

Van Stone, James W. and Wendell H. Oswalt. *The Caribou Eskimos of Eskimo Point*. Department of Indian and Northern Affairs and National Resources, Northern Co-ordination and Research Centre, 1952.

von Finckenstein, Maria. "John Pangnark, 1920-1980." *Inuit Art Quarterly* 13, no. 1 (Spring 1998): 26-31.

The Winnipeg Art Gallery. *Eskimo Point/Arviat*. Winnipeg: The Winnipeg Art Gallery, 1982.

RANKIN INLET

Smith, Dale Wik. "A Keewatin Story: Cultural Revolution in the North." *Chronicle* (Winter 1977): 8-12.

Swinton, George. *Tiktak: Sculptor from Rankin Inlet, N.W.T.* Winnipeg: Gallery 1.1.1., University of Manitoba, 1970.

Swinton, George. "The Sculptor Tiktak." *artscanada* no. 144/145 (June 1970): 47.

The Winnipeg Art Gallery. *Rankin Inlet: Kangirlliniq*. Essays by Bernadette Driscoll, Dr. Robert G. Williamson, Stanley Zazelenchuk, and Nancy E. Newman. Winnipeg: The Winnipeg Art Gallery, 1981.

Zazelenchuk, Stanley. "Kavik: The Man and the Artist." *Arts and Culture of the North* 4, no. 2 (Spring 1980): 219, 222.

Zazelenchuk, Stanley. "The Mother and Child Sculpture of Tiktak." *Arts and Culture of the North* 4, no. 3 (Summer 1980): 265.

REPULSE BAY

Ernerk, Peter. "Repulse Bay." *The Nunavut Handbook*. Iqaluit: Nortext Multimedia Inc., 1998, p. 258-263.

Trafford Bissett, Diana. "Notes on the History of Carving in Repulse Bay." Unpublished paper, The Winnipeg Art Gallery files, 1973.

von Finckenstein, Maria. "Curator's Choice: John Kaunak." *Inuit Art Quarterly* 15, no. 1 (Spring 2000): 32-36.

The Winnipeg Art Gallery. *John Kaunak, an Artist from Repulse Bay*. Brochure for exhibition. Winnipeg: The Winnipeg Art Gallery, 1973.

The Winnipeg Art Gallery. *Repulse Bay*. Winnipeg: The Winnipeg Art Gallery, 1978.

BAKER LAKE ᖃᒪᓂᑦᑐᐊᖅ

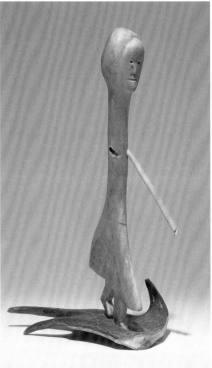

MOSES AKILAK, b. 1932
ᒧᓯᔅ ᐊᑭᓚᒃ
Baker Lake ᖃᒪᓂᑦᑐᐊᖅ
Woman, 1960s
stone
38.3 x 18.3 x 16.8
699.71

MARTHA TIKTAQ ANAUTALIK
1928-1994
ᒫᑕ ᑎᒃᑕᖅ ᐊᓇᐅᑕᓕᒃ
Baker Lake ᖃᒪᓂᑦᑐᐊᖅ
Walking Woman, 1967
antler
29.6 x 20 x 13
773.71

THOMAS SIVURAQ, b. 1941
ᓴᒥᔅ ᔨᐳᕋᖅ
Baker Lake ᖃᒪᓂᑐᐊᖅ
Kneeling Mother with Child,
1960s
stone
30 x 34.5 x 27.2
630.71

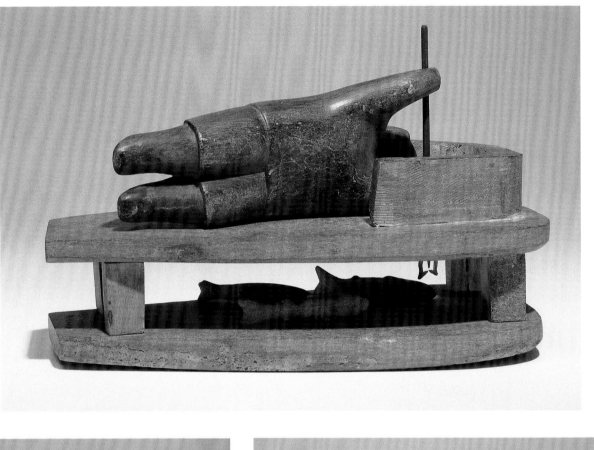

PAULI ARNARKYUINAQ
1926-1990
ᐸᑦ ᐊˢᏗᗩᐃᐁᑫᓄᖅ
Baker Lake ˢᏏᏓ ᓇᑕ ᐊ ᖅ
Ice Fishing Scene, 1960s
stone, horn, wood, sinew
11.2 x 23.1 x 13.3
643.71

VITAL MAKPAAQ, 1922-1978
ᐱᑕᒐ ᒪ ᑫᐸᖅ
Baker Lake ˢᏏᏓ ᓇᑕ ᐊ ᖅ
Fisherman, 1960s
stone, bone
18.2 x 10.1 x 13.3
606.71

LUKE ANGUHADLUQ
1895-1982
ᓗᖅ ᐊ ᖅ ᐅᒐᑦ ᓗᖅ
Baker Lake ˢᏏᏓ ᓇᑕ ᐊ ᖅ
Caribou, c. 1963
stone
11.8 x 26.3 x 5.8
588.71

JAMES KINGILIK, 1912-1975
ᔭᐃᓪ ᑭᖕᒋᓕᒃ
Baker Lake ᖃᒪᓂᑦᑐᐊᖅ
Muskox, 1960
stone, horn
16.5 x 21.7 x 8.7
691.71

VITAL MAKPAAQ, 1922-1978
ᐱᑖᑦ ᒪᒃᐸᖅ
Baker Lake ᖃᒪᓂᑦᑐᐊᖅ
Caribou Scratching, c. 1960
stone
12.9 x 18 x 11.1
608.71

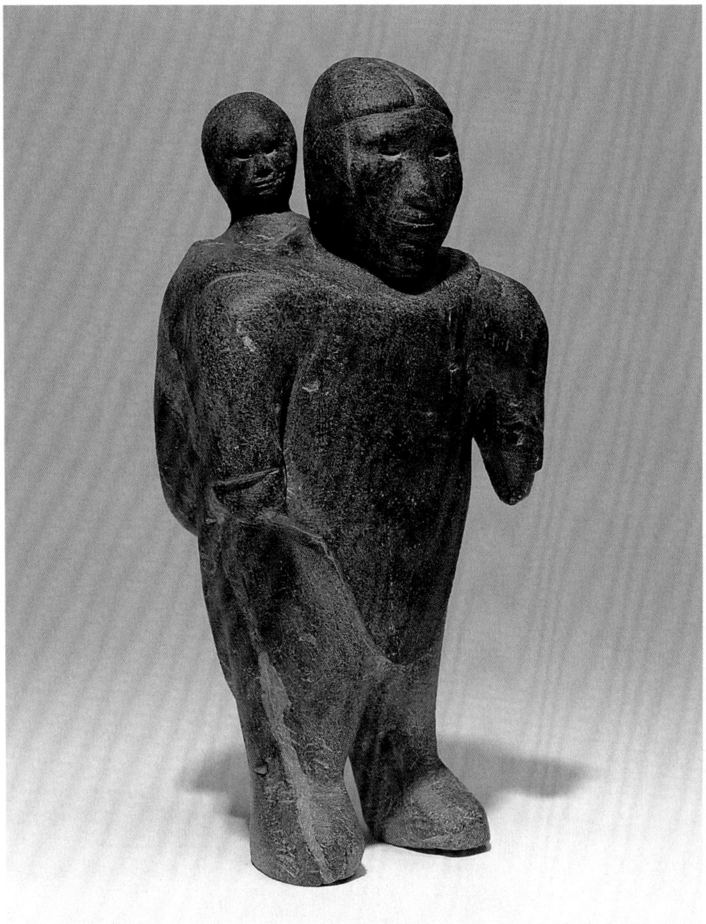

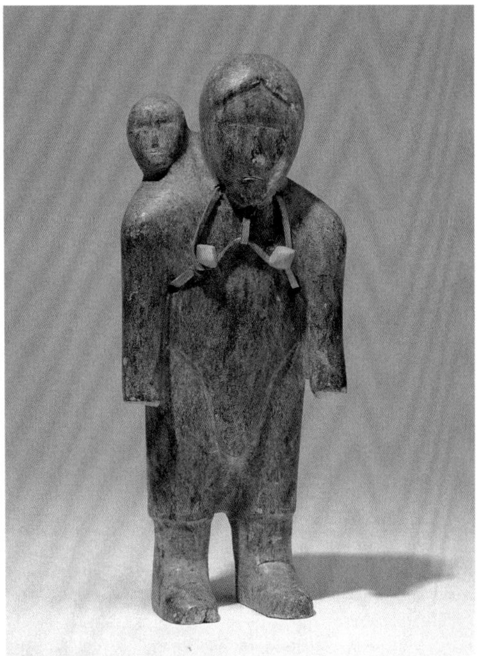

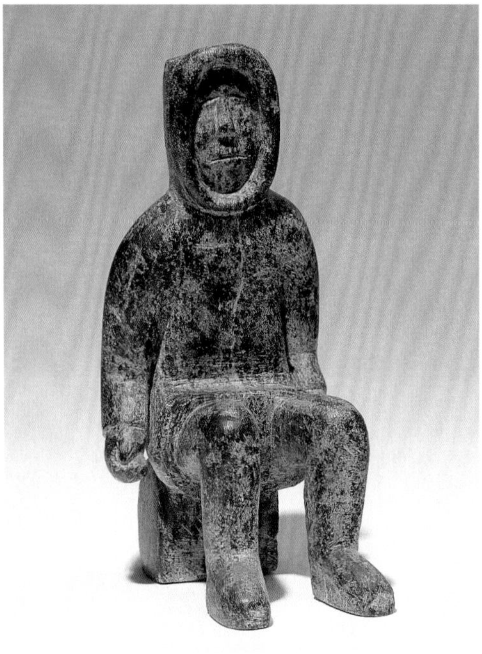

MARTHA APTANIK, 1915-1972
ᒫᑕ ᐊᑉᑕᓂᒃ
Baker Lake ᖃᒪᓂᑦᑐᐊᖅ
Mother and Child, 1960s
stone
20.8 x 10.6 x 10.1
629.71

NOAH ANGNATARATUK
1900-Unknown
ᓄᐊ ᐊᖕᓇᑕᕋᑐᒃ
Baker Lake ᖃᒪᓂᑦᑐᐊᖅ
Mother and Child, c. 1963
stone, skin, ivory
21.3 x 9 x 8.2
775.71

MARY YUUSIPIK SINGAQTI
b. 1936
ᒥᐅᕆ ᔫᓯᐱᒃ ᓯᖕᒐᖅᑎ
Baker Lake ᖃᒪᓂᑦᑐᐊᖅ
Man Sitting on Box, 1960s
stone
13.2 x 6.3 x 7.9
709.71

VITAL MAKPAAQ, 1922-1978
ᐱᑖᓪ ᒪᒃᐹᖅ
Baker Lake ᕃᒪᓂᑐᐋᖅ
Woman Carrying Pail, 1960s
stone
20.1 x 14.5 x 8.3
785.71

SILAS QIYUK, b. 1933
ᓴᐃᓚᔅ ᕿᔪᒃ
Baker Lake ᖃᒪᓂᑦᑐᐊᖅ
Mother and Child, c. 1963
stone
13.4 x 4.8 x 3.2
764.71

GEORGE TATANNIQ, 1910-1991
ᔪᐊᒋ ᑕᑕᓂᖅ
Baker Lake ᖃᒪᓂᑦᑐᐊᖅ
Mother and Two Children,
c. 1963
stone
20.4 x 5.7 x 7.6
649.71

FRANCIS KALURAQ, 1931-1990
ᑕᕋᓐᓯᔅ ᑲᓗᕋᖅ
Baker Lake ᖃᒪᓂᑦᑐᐊᖅ
Woman on One Knee, c. 1963
stone, antler
21.5 x 13.8 x 21.2
584.71

GEORGE TATANNIQ, 1910-1991
ᐸᐊᒃ ᑕᑕᓂᖅ
Baker Lake ᖃᒪᓂᑐᐊᖅ
Muskox, 1963
stone, antler
13.8 x 22 x 6.2
648.71

DAVID IKUUTAQ, 1926-1984
ᑕᐃᕕᑦ ᐃᑯᑕᖅ
Baker Lake ᖃᒪᓂᖅᒍᓂᖅ
Bear Shaman, 1960s
stone
18.6 x 11.4 x 5.5
2184.71

ARVIAT ⊲ˤ∆⊲ᶜ

**MARGO ATATLOAK
ANGNAYUINAK**, b. 1919
ĹJ ⊲ᶜⵑˤᵇ ⊲ˤₐᣔᐃᵃₐˤᵇ
Arviat ⊲ˤ∆⊲ᶜ
*Man with Bound Head and
Bird*, 1969
stone, sinew
14.5 x 16.7 x 12.9
1516.71

MARC ALIKASWA, b. 1928
Ĺᵇ ⊲ᗈᑯᐅ
Arviat ⊲ˤ∆⊲ᶜ
Seated Mother with Child, 1969
stone
18.7 x 13.7 x 18.7
1290.71

SIMON KATSUAK, 1911-1972
ᐦ∆Ĺᵃ ᑲᶜᑯ⊲ˤᵇ
Arviat ⊲ˤ∆⊲ᶜ
Mother Nursing Child, 1968
stone, antler
16.8 x 18.1 x 8.6
1326.71

GEORGE ARLUK, b. 1949
ᐸᐊᑊ ᐋᔅᘁᕁ
Arviat ᐊᕁᐊᐊᑊ
Shaman, c. 1970
whalebone, antler, wood
46.6 x 30.9 x 28.2
2112.71

YAHA ANGNAYUINAK, b. 1907
ᔕᕼᐊ ᐊᖬᐁᕉᐊᖬᐊᖅ
Arviat ᐊᕐᐱᐊᑦ
Mother and Children, 1969
stone
13.3 x 5 x 10.1
1511.71

MADELAIN KATOO PAMEOK
b. 1916
ᒪᑕᓚᐃ ᑲᑐ ᐸᒥᐅᖅ
Arviat ᐊᕐᐱᐊᑦ
Mother with Child on Knee,
1967
stone
19.1 x 16.6 x 6.4
1190.71

JOHN PANGNARK, 1920-1980
ᔮᓐ ᐸᖕᓇᖅ
Arviat ᐊᕐᐱᐊᑦ
Seated Figure, 1968
stone
12.8 x 7 x 13.3
1249.71

JOHN PANGNARK, 1920-1980
ᔮᓐ ᐸᖕᓇᖅ
Arviat ᐊᕐᐱᐊᑦ
Mother and Child, 1969
stone
14.1 x 7.3 x 14.7
1265.71

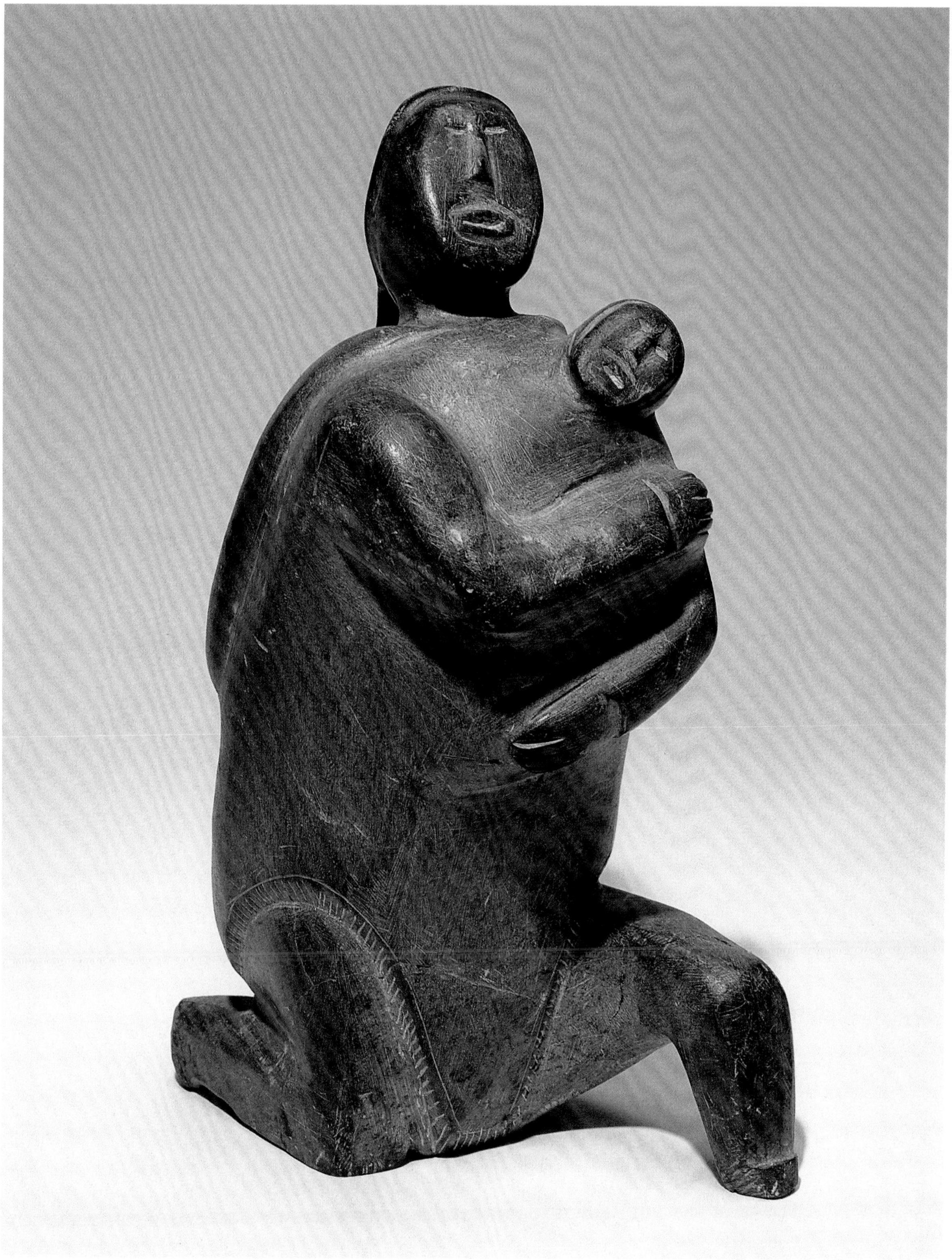

MARGARET UYAUPERQ ANIKSAK
1905-1993
ᒫᒍᓂᑦ ᐅᔭᐃᐱᖅ ᐊᓂᒃᓴᖅ
Arviat ᐊᕐᕕᐊᑦ
Mother and Child, 1969
stone
28.6 x 12.3 x 17.5
1192.71

LUCY TASSEOR TUTSWEETOK
b. 1934
ᒍᖅ ᑕᑕᐅᖅ ᑐᑕᐱᐊᑐᖅ
Arviat ᐊᕐᐱᐊᑦ
Mother and Children, 1960s
stone
47 x 15.8 x 27.8
1428.71

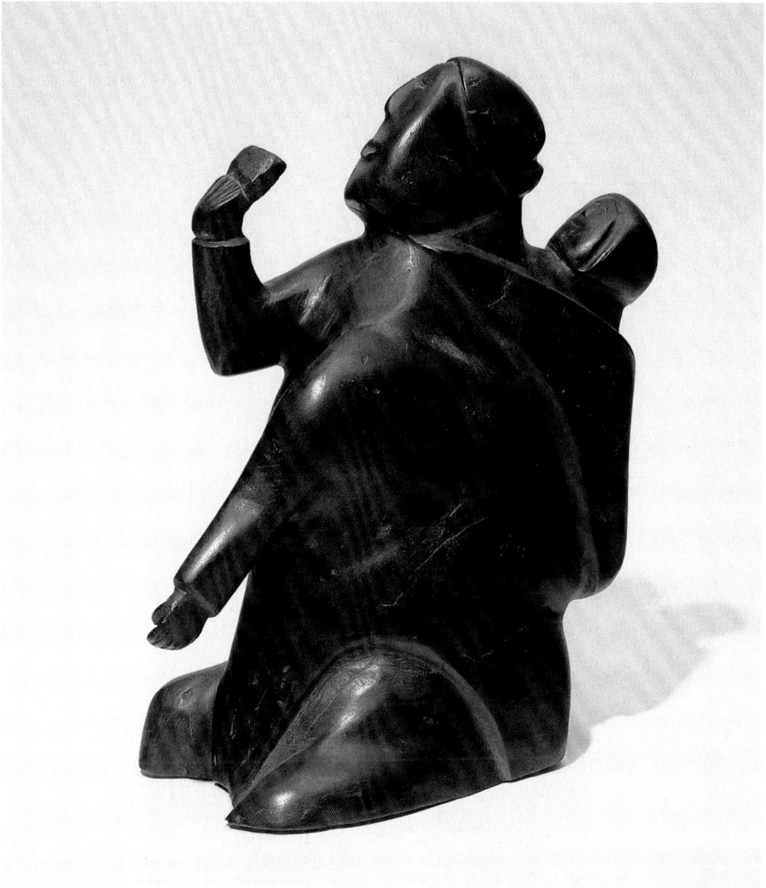

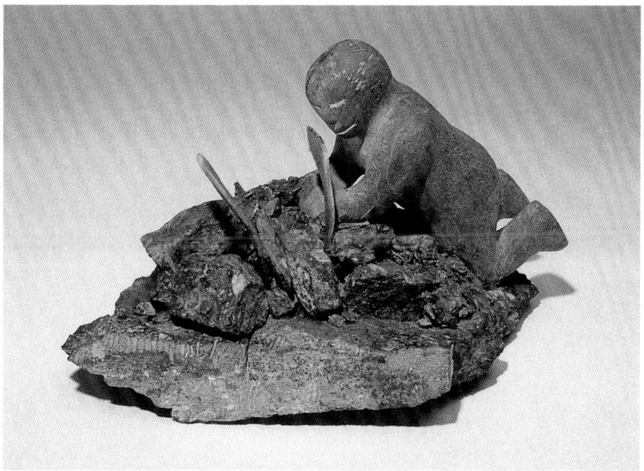

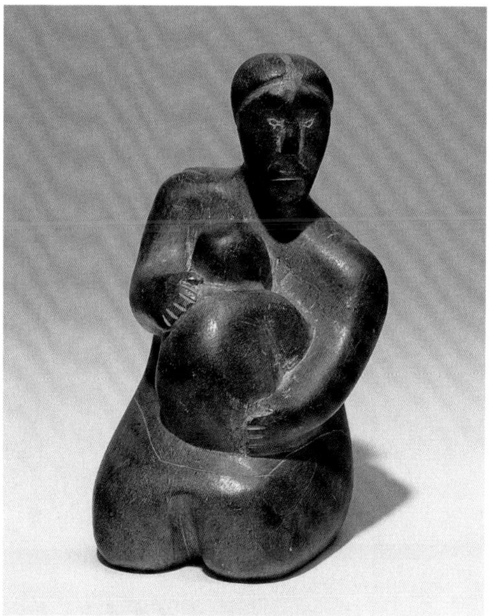

MARGARET UYAUPERQ ANIKSAK, 1905-1993
ᒫᒍᓇᑦ ᐅᔭᐃᐱᖅ ᐊᓂᒃᓴᖅ
Arviat ᐊᕐᕕᐊᑦ
Mother Eating, 1969
27.4 x 12 x 22.5
1193.71

JOHN KUKSUK, 1923-1969
ᔩᓐ ᖁᒃᓱᒃ
Arviat ᐊᕐᕕᐊᑦ
Man Building Caribou Cache, 1967
stone, antler
13.3 x 23.6 x 19.5
1202.71

ANDY MAMGARK, 1930-1997
ᐋᓐᑎ ᒪᒻᖓᖅ
Arviat ᐊᕐᕕᐊᑦ
Mother and Child, 1969
stone
16.3 x 10.3 x 11.5
1316.71

JACOB IRKOK, b. 1937
ᔅᐱᑲᐸᑦ ᐃᕐᑯᑉ
Arviat ᐊᕐᕕᐊᑦ
Man Beating Dog, 1968
antler, sinew
28 x 21.4 x 8.9
1382.71

HENRY ISLUANIK, b. 1925
ᕼᐊᔭᕋᓇ ᐃᔪᐊᓂᑉ
Arviat ᐊᕐᕕᐊᑦ
*Herd of Caribou Pursued by
Wolf*, 1966
antler
11.2 x 38.5 x 20.9
1554.71

PETER KOMAK, 1911-1984
ᐲᑕ ᑯᒪᖅ
Arviat ᐊᕐᕕᐊᑦ
Faces of Mother and Child,
1968-1969
antler, baleen
24.3 x 19.5 x 31.7
1591.71

JOHN ATTOK, 1906-1980
ᔪᐊ ᐊᑐᖅ
Arviat ᐊᕐᕕᐊᑦ
Man and Bird, 1969
whalebone, antler
15.9 x 10.2 x 8.2
1221.71

RANKIN INLET ᑲᖕᒋᖅᓚᓂᖅ

ELI TIKEAYAK, b. 1933
ᐃᓕ ᑎᑭᐊᔭᒃ
Rankin Inlet ᑲᖕᒋᖅᓚᓂᖅ
Man with Raised Arm, 1963
stone
10.1 x 7.3 x 3.8
2087.71

JOHN TIKTAK, 1916-1981
ᔮᓐ ᑎᒃᑕᖅ
Rankin Inlet ᑲᖕᒋᖅᓚᓂᖅ
Mother and Child, 1960s
stone
13 x 8.9 x 8.6
2061.71

JOHN TIKTAK, 1916-1981
ᔮᓐ ᑎᒃᑕᖅ
Rankin Inlet ᑲᖕᒋᖅᓚᓂᖅ
Seated Man, 1963-1964
stone
13.6 x 8.5 x 11.5
2059.71

MICHAEL ANGUTITUAK, b. 1912
ᒪᐃᑦ ᐊᖏᑎᑐᐊᖅ
Rankin Inlet ᖃᒪᓂᖅᒃᑐᓂᖅ
Man's Head, 1960s
stone
22.2 x 12.4 x 12.1
2172.71

THOMAS UGJUK, b. 1921
ᑖᒫ ᐊᒡᔪᒃ
Rankin Inlet ᖃᒪᓂᖅᒃᑐᓂᖅ
Woman, 1960s
stone
12.4 x 8 x 4.3
782.71

SHERKTANAK ANIKSAK, b. 1911
ᔪᖅᑕᓇᖅ ᐊᓂᒃᓴᖅ
Rankin Inlet ᖃᒪᓂᖅᒃᑐᓂᖅ
Hooded Head of a Man, 1960s
stone, fur
16.1 x 7 x 11.9
2176.71

JOHN TIKTAK, 1916-1981
ᒃᓇ ᑎᒃᑕᖅ
Rankin Inlet ᑲᖕᒋᖅᒃᓗᓂᖅ
Woman and Child, 1960s
stone
16 x 5.6 x 8.8
2060.71

REPULSE BAY ᐊᐅᐸᑦ

JOHN KAUNAK, b. 1941
ᔮᓐ ᖃᐅᓇᖅ
Repulse Bay ᐊᐅᐸᑦ
*Hunter and Dogs Chasing
Polar Bear*, 1966
stone, antler, colouring
11.1 x 41 x 10.7
3090.71

JOHN KAUNAK, b. 1941
ᔮᓐ ᖃᐅᓇᖅ
Repulse Bay ᐊᐅᐸᑦ
Hunter Harpooning Seal, 1966
stone, antler, sinew, ivory
18.6 x 11.5 x 11.3
3091.71

JOHN KAUNAK, b. 1941
ᔮᓐ ᖃᐅᓇᖅ
Repulse Bay ᐊᐅᐸᑦ
Archer, 1966
stone, antler, sinew
9.6 x 10.2 x 7.8
3092.71

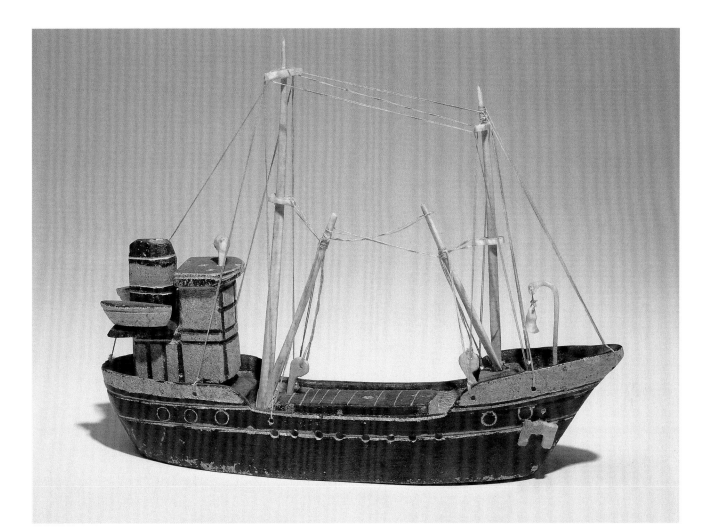

JOHN KAUNAK, b. 1941
ᐴᵃ ᖃᐅᓇᖅ
Repulse Bay ᐊᐅᔭᑦ
Whaling Boat, 1967
stone, string, ivory, shoe
polish
16 x 20.5 x 5.2
3045.71

MARK TUNGILIK, 1913-1986
ᒫᖅ ᑐᖕᒋᓕᒃ
Repulse Bay ᐊᐅᔭᑦ
Caribou, prior to 1971
stone, bone
7.1 x 15.8 x 3.8
2294.71

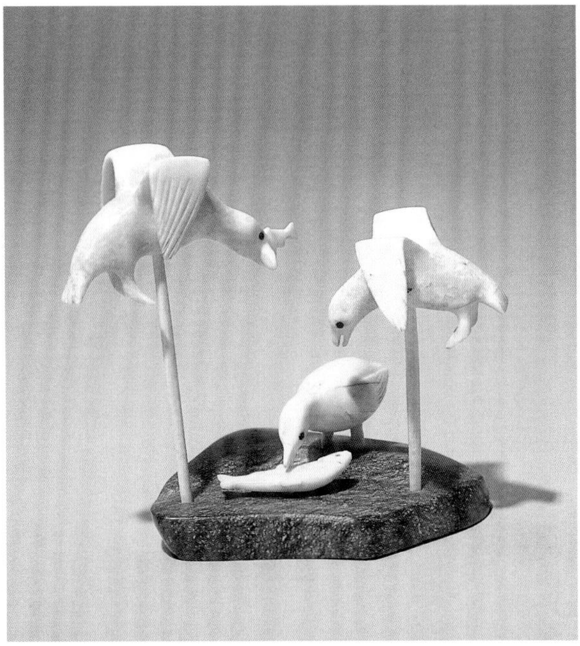

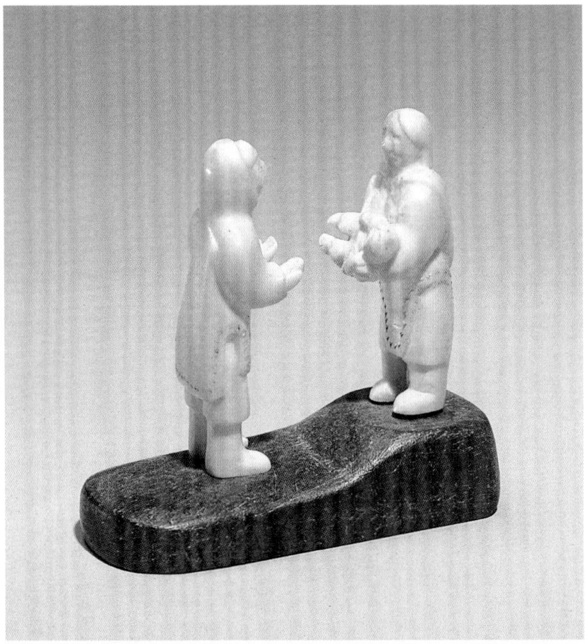

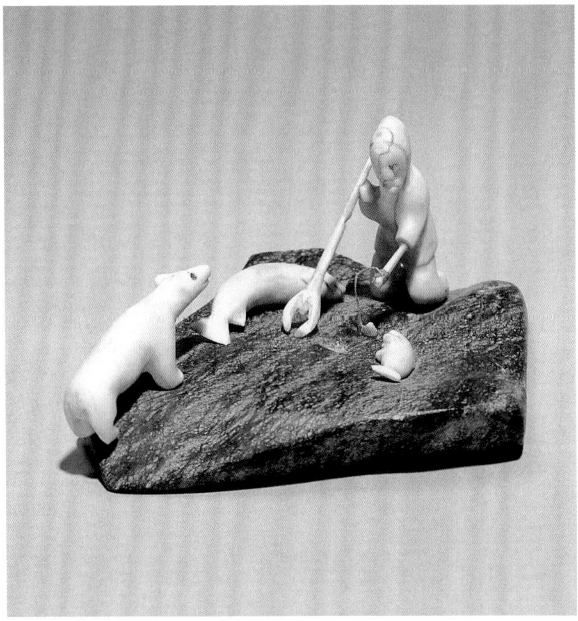

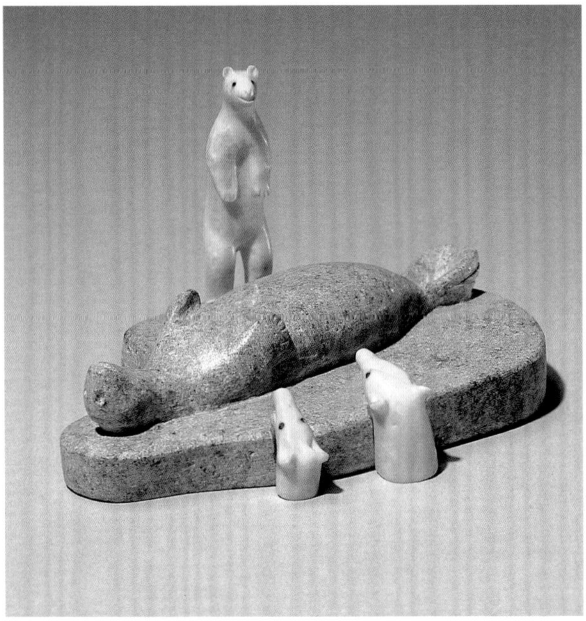

MADELEINE ISSERKUT KRINGAYARK, 1928-1986
ᒫᑕᓚᓐ ᐃᓯᖅᑯᑦ ᕿᖕᒐᔭᖅ
Repulse Bay ᓇᐅᔮᑦ
Birds with Fish, prior to 1971
stone, ivory, baleen
9.2 x 10.5 x 8
2568.71

ABRAHAM TEEGONAK, b. 1926
ᐄᐳᕋᒻ ᑎᒍᓇᒃ
Repulse Bay ᓇᐅᔮᑦ
Couple with Child, c. 1966
stone, ivory, shoe polish
5.9 x 6.2 x 3
2996.71

CELINA SEELEENAK PUTULIK
b. 1934
ᓯᓕᓇ ᓯᓕᓇᖅ ᐳᑐᓕᒃ
Repulse Bay ᓇᐅᔮᑦ
Fisherman Approached by Polar Bear, prior to 1971
stone, ivory
3.9 x 9.4 x 7.5
3443.71

JAKI NANORDLUK, b. 1937
ᔮᑭ ᓇᓄᕐᓗᒃ
Repulse Bay ᓇᐅᔮᑦ
Bears Investigating Dead Seal, prior to 1971
stone, ivory
6.4 x 10.8 x 8.2
2862.71

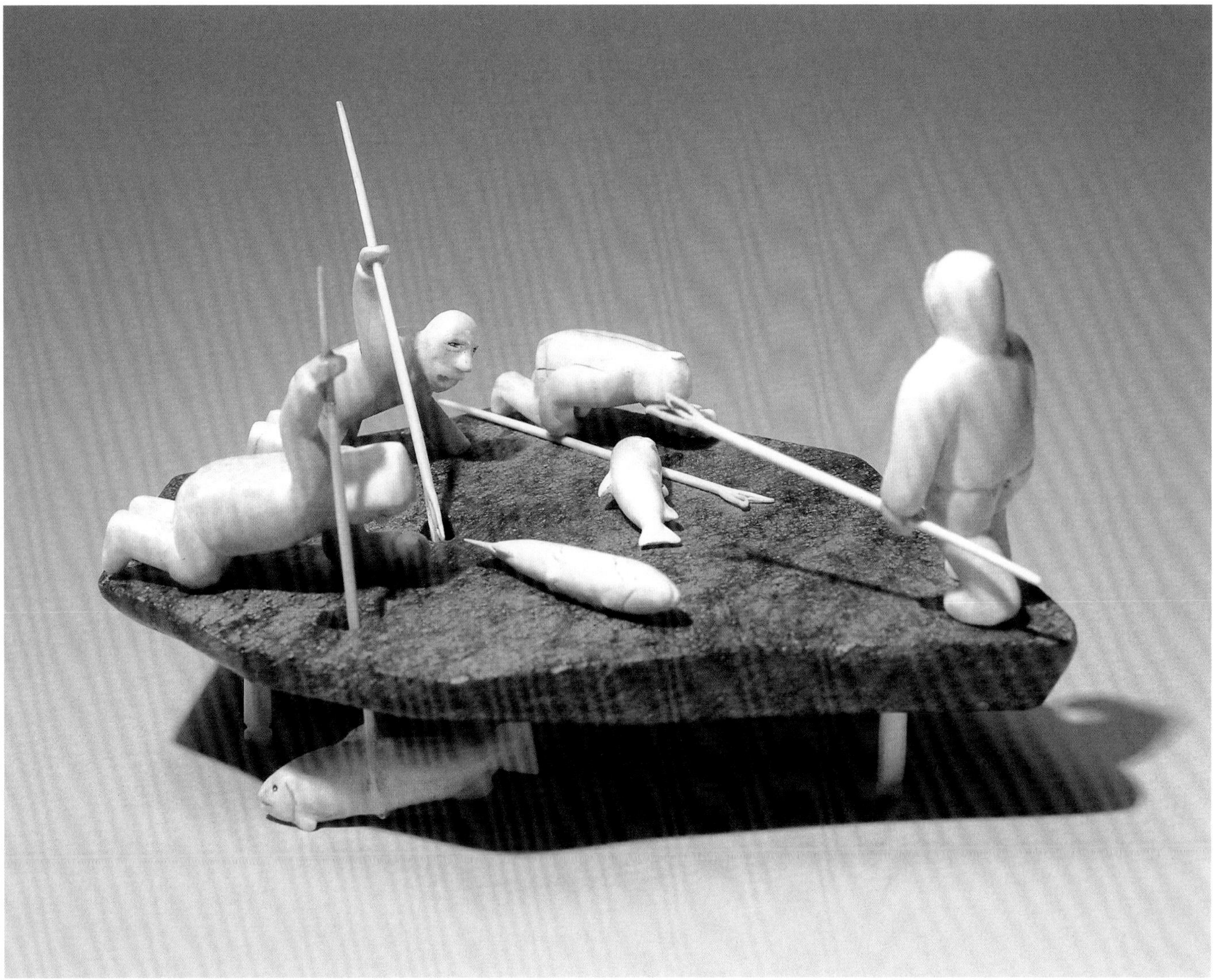

MARK TUNGILIK, 1913-1986
ᒫᒃ ᑐᖏᓕᒃ
Repulse Bay ᓇᐅᔮᑦ
Ice Fishing, prior to 1971
stone, ivory, sinew, graphite?
8.5 x 15.2 x 13.1
2312.71

110

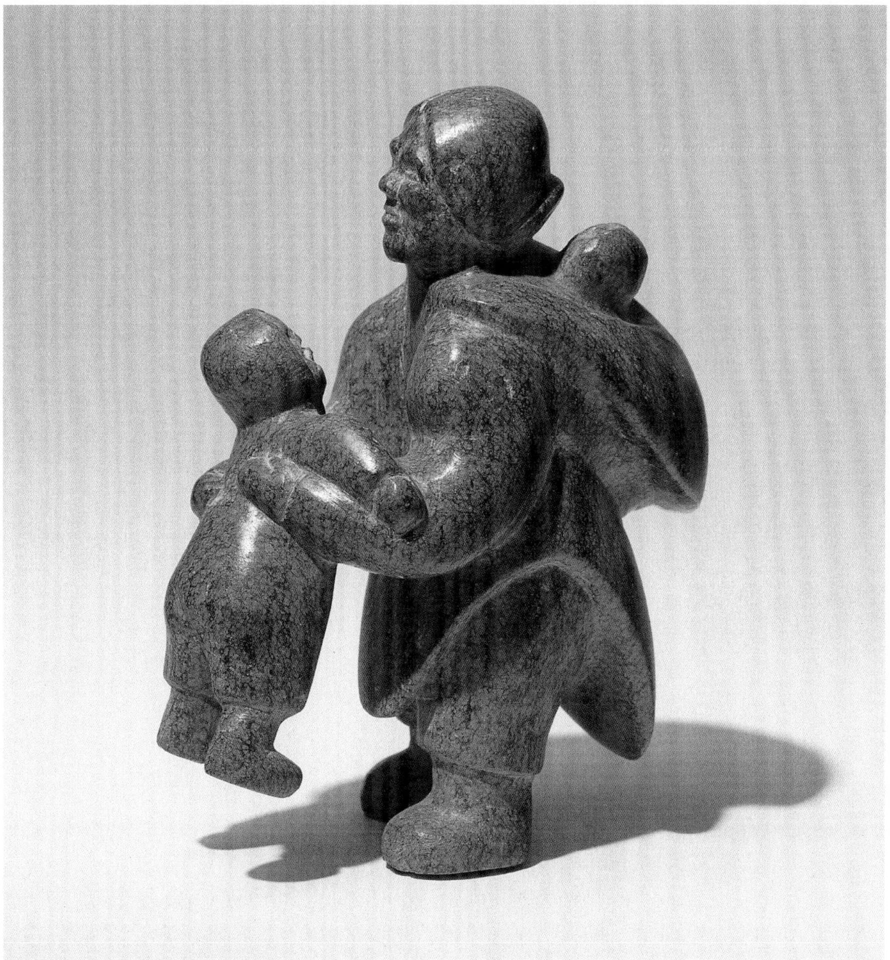

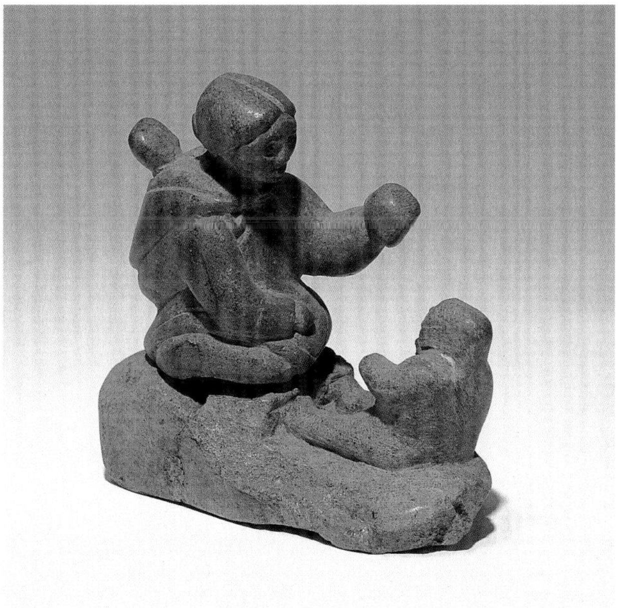

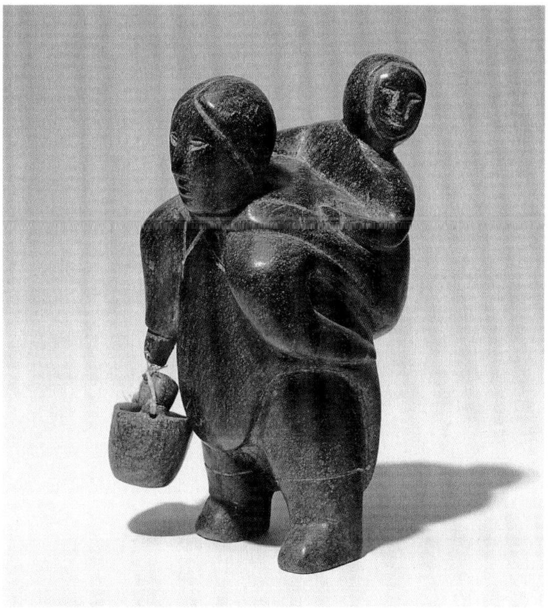

LOUISE ANGUATSIARK TUNGILIK, 1917-1988
ᓗᐃᔅ ᐊᖑᐊᑦᓯᐊᖅ ᑐᖏᓕᒃ
Repulse Bay ᓇᐅᔮᑦ
Woman and Children,
prior to 1971
stone
12.5 x 5.9 x 9.3
2323.71

MARIA MAPSALAK, b. 1950
ᒪᕆᐊ ᒪᑉᓴᓚᒃ
Repulse Bay ᓇᐅᔮᑦ
Mother and Child Playing Catch, prior to 1971
stone
8.7 x 9 x 4.7
2831.71

THERESE PAOLAK TUGUMIAR
b. 1944
ᑎᕆᓯ ᐸᐅᓚᒃ ᑐᒍᒥᐊᖅ
Repulse Bay ᓇᐅᔮᑦ
Mother Carrying Bucket, 1963
stone, sinew
13.3 x 7.5 x 7.6
3567.71

112

MARIANO AUPILLARDJUK
b. 1923
ᒪᕆᐊᓄ ᐊᐆᐱᓚᕐᔪᒃ
Repulse Bay ᓇᐅᔮᑦ
Hunter at Seal Breathing Hole,
prior to 1971
stone, ivory, sinew
14 x 10.7 x 11.5
2456.71

CHRISTINE AALUK
SIVANERTOK, b. 1938
ᑯᕆᔅᑏᓇ ᐋᓗᒃ ᓯᕚᓂᕐᑐᖅ
Repulse Bay ᓇᐅᔮᑦ
Woman's Tattooed Face, prior to
1971
stone, sinew
24.6 x 15.5 x 8.5
3221.71

IRENE KATAK ANGUTITAQ
1914-1971
ᐊᐃᕆᐣ ᑲᑕᒃ ᐊᖕᒍᑎᑕᖅ
Repulse Bay ᓇᐅᔮᑦ
Mother and Child, 1964
stone
7.5 x 7.5 x 7.6
2786.71

Index of Artists

List of Artists in The Twomey Collection

Community	Artist's Name	Birth/ Death	Disc Number	Family Number	# of Works
Akulivik	Qingali, Killupa	1934	E9-711		1
Akulivik	Qullialu, Makusikalla Aliqu	1930-1989	E9-1309	Puv-34, H	2
Arctic Bay	Akitirq, Atoat	1935	E5-199	AB-13, W	15
Arctic Bay	Akitirq, Pauloosie	1935	E5-90	AB-13, H	22
Arctic Bay	Akpaliapik, Lazaroosee	1921	E5-907	AB-47, H	2
Arctic Bay	Akpaliapik, Nakyuraq	1922	E5-908	AB-47, W	3
Arctic Bay	Alooloo, Elisapee Kanangnaq	1918-1985	E5-234	AB-12, W	19
Arctic Bay	Alooloo, Nashook	1948	E5-917	AB-12, S	7
Arctic Bay	Alooloo, Peter	1908-1994	E5-88	AB-12, H	25
Arctic Bay	Aola, Pakkak	1909	E5-160	AB-24, W	3
Arctic Bay	Arnauyumayuq, Joseph	1927	E5-76	AB-08, H	1
Arctic Bay	Attagutsiak, Issiah	1918	E5-379	AB-34, H	1
Arctic Bay	Eenooahrak	1947	E5-910	AB-33, S/S	2
Arctic Bay	Eenoya, Morty	1957	E5-1173	AB-12, D	1
Arctic Bay	Ejangiaq, Paul	1918	E5-915	AB-22, S	1
Arctic Bay	Enoogoo, Zebedee	1931	E5-243	AB-32, H	3
Arctic Bay	Ettuk, Jimmy	1908-1975	E5-213	AB-27, H	1
Arctic Bay	Ettuk, Martha Aqiqqaqjuk	1911	E5-214	AB-27, W	2
Arctic Bay	Evalak, Koopinoak	1901	E5-83	AB-09, H	1
Arctic Bay	Evvala, Esigaituk	1956	E5-1160	AB-15, D	1
Arctic Bay	Evvala, Mary Qumangapik	1959	E5-1436	AB-15, D	1
Arctic Bay	Evvala, Paneloo	1953	E5-1135	AB-15, D	1
Arctic Bay	Innotik, Attagootak	1929	E5-94	AB-33, W	32
Arctic Bay	Inootik (Innutiq?), George	1926	E5-220	AB-30, H	1
Arctic Bay	Issuqangituq, Rebecca	1936	E4-255	AB-04, W	5
Arctic Bay	Issuqangituq, David	1937	E5-57	AB-04, H	9
Arctic Bay	Kanayuk, Seemee	1938	E5-104	AB-17, H	1
Arctic Bay	Kigutikakjuk, Ikey	1942	E5-121	AB-23, H	2
Arctic Bay	Kigutikakjuk, Olajuk	1943	E5-92	AB-23, W	1
Arctic Bay	Koonayook, Agluk	1924	E5-119	AB-22, W	1
Arctic Bay	Koonoo, Aibilli	1940	E5-248	AB-33, S	5
Arctic Bay	Koonook, John	1939	E5-91	AB-14, H	6
Arctic Bay	Kuppaq, Elijah	1903-1979	E5-64	AB-06, H	4
Arctic Bay	Mosesie	1956	E5-1165	AB-33, S/S	1
Arctic Bay	Muckpa, Pauloosie	1937	E5-909	AB-48, H	7
Arctic Bay	Muckpa, Qumangapik	1939	E5-235	AB-48, W	9
Arctic Bay	Muckpaloo, Koonoo	1939	E5-904	AB-31, W	1
Arctic Bay	Napachee-Kadlak, Leah Qamanirq	1934	E4-254	AB-01, W	5
Arctic Bay	Napachee-Kadlak, Samwillie Boaz	1950	E5-1114	AB-01, S	2
Arctic Bay	Naqitaqvik, Martha Erkasak	1944	E5-906	AB-10, W	4
Arctic Bay	Naqitaqvik, Olayuq	1943	E5-86	AB-10, H	10
Arctic Bay	Ochitok, Jootah	1947	E5-913	AB-08, S/S	3
Arctic Bay	Oqallak, Joseph	1940	E5-218	AB-29, H	3
Arctic Bay	Oyukuluk, Koonoo	1946	E5-113	AB-19, S	1
Arctic Bay	Panapuk, Sangooya	1935	E5-215	AB-28, H	1
Arctic Bay	Phillip, Lew	1947	E5-911	AB-45, S	24
Arctic Bay	Qamanirq, Benjamin Natsiq	1955	E5-1146	AB-46, S	2
Arctic Bay	Qamanirq, Paniluk	1935	E5-244	AB-46, W	32
Arctic Bay	Qamanirq, Philip	1933	E5-902	AB-46, H	6
Arctic Bay	Qamanirq, Simon	1953	E5-1131	AB-46, S	2
Arctic Bay	Qaunaq, Sakiassee	1924	E5-82	AB-34, A/S	5
Arctic Bay	Sangooyak, Singooree	1925	E5-720	AB-38, H (widow)	1
Arctic Bay	Taqtu, Imaruituq	1934	E5-903	AB-20, W	4
Arctic Bay	Taqtu, Juda	1937	E5-110	AB-20, H	5
Arctic Bay	Tattatuapik, Ezra	1956	E5-1164	AB-40, S	1
Arctic Bay	Tattatuapik, Sanguya	1949	E5-929	AB-32, D	3
Arctic Bay	Tattatuapik, Tommy	1937	E5-876	AB-40, H	6
Arctic Bay	Toongalook	1912-1967	E5-900	AB-45, H	3
Arctic Bay	Tunraluk, Tuqaq	1915	E5-901	AB-45, W	1
Arviat	Akadlaka, Marcel	1911	E1-153	AR-38, H	1
Arviat	Akammuk, Alice Sakitnak	1940	E1-260	AR-26, W	5
Arviat	Akatsiak, Meda	1925	E1-186	AR-27, W	10
Arviat	Alareak, Edward	1927	E1-086	?	2
Arviat	Alareak, Elizabeth Kingaruyak	1943	E1-227	AR-19, W	1
Arviat	Alikaswa, Marc	1928	E1-121	AR-29, H	7
Arviat	Amak, Leo	1945	E1-200	AR-50, H	1
Arviat	Anarauyak, George	1897-1988	E1-093	AR-21, H	1
Arviat	Angatajuak, Angelina	1936	E1-313	AR-38, W	1
Arviat	Angmak, Theresa Alunak	1926	E1-530	AR-101, W	5
Arviat	Angnayuinak, Margo Atatloak	1919	E1-476	AR-93, W	11
Arviat	Angnayuinak, Yaha	1907	E1-475	AR-93, H	3
Arviat	Anoee, Eric	1924-1989	E1-264	AR-68, H	1
Arviat	Anoee, Martina Pissuyui	1933	E1-148	AR-68, W	3
Arviat	Anowtalik, Luke	1932	E1-524	AR-100, H	10
Arviat	Anowtalik, Mary Ayaq	1938	E1-447	AR-100, W	5
Arviat	Aqiaq, John	1913	E1-305	AR-74, H	2
Arviat	Arluk, George	1949	E3-1049	RI-24, S	38
Arviat	Arnayuinak, Thomas	1931-1973	E1-261	AR-66, H	11
Arviat	Attok, John	1906-1980	E1-83	AR-20, H	8
Arviat	Aulatjut, Elizabeth Nutaraluk	1914-1998	E1-445	AR-89, W	23
Arviat	Eekerkik, Romeo	1923-1983	E1-066	AR-17, H	4
Arviat	Eetak, Martha Mokjunik	1907	E1-055	AR-13, W	9
Arviat	Hallauk, Joy Kiluvigyuak	1940-2000	E1-366	AR-81, W	9
Arviat	Hallauk, Luke	1931-1994	E1-039	AR-9, Ba	1
Arviat	Hanna, David	1940	E1-374	AR-82, H	1
Arviat	Illungiak, Nicolas	1959	E1-774	AR-68, S/S	1
Arviat	Iootna, Edward	1926	E1-368	AR-80, H	5
Arviat	Iplaut, Anita	1937	E1-125	AR-11, W	1
Arviat	Iqlu, Annie	1945	E1-474	AR-67, S/D	1
Arviat	Irkok, Eulalie Utuuyak	1935	E1-149	AR-69, W	4
Arviat	Irkok, Jacob	1937	E1-271	AR-69, H	9
Arviat	Isluanik, Akupirniq	1932	E1-491	AR-95, W	2
Arviat	Isluanik, Henry	1925	E1-489	AR-95, H	1
Arviat	Issumatarjuak, David	1929	E1-097	AR-22, H	2
Arviat	Issumatarjuak, Martha Anarosuk	1935	E1-064	AR-22, W	2
Arviat	Katsuak, Simon	1911-1972	E1-193	AR-48, H	3
Arviat	Kaurajuk, Joe	1942	E1-370	AR-81, H	13
Arviat	Kaviok, Joanni	1926	E1-301	AR-73, H	2
Arviat	Komak, Peter	1911-1984	E1-237	AR-60, H	6
Arviat	Koomak, Martha Apsaitok	1944	E1-199	AR-60, W	4
Arviat	Kopanuak, Monique	1913-1987	E1-194	AR-48, W	8
Arviat	Kovakak, Kaikai Noah	1908	E1-263	AR-67, H	1
Arviat	Kovakak, Margaret Angaksatsiak	1951	E1-603	AR-67, S/D	3
Arviat	Kovakak, Mary Kigerk	1908-1971	E1-472	AR-67, W	1

Community	Artist's Name	Birth/Death	Disc Number	Family Number	# of Works
Arviat	Kowgayuk, Rhoda Eegie	1947	E1-375	AR-26, A/D	1
Arviat	Kriniksi, Luke	1938	E1-198	AR-49, H	1
Arviat	Kuksuk, John	1923-1969	E1-043	AR-10, H	1
Arviat	Mamgark, Andy	1930-1997	E1-164	AR-44, H	1
Arviat	Mamgark, Eva Seuteruk	1933	E1-196	AR-44, W	2
Arviat	Manik, Catherine Amak	1942	E1-150	AR-46, W	6
Arviat	Miki, Andy	1918-1983	E1-436	AR-88, H	8
Arviat	Mukyungnik, Eve Ukanak	1941	E1-477	AR-90, W	3
Arviat	Nauksaut, Daniel	1924	E1-300	AR-72, H	1
Arviat	Nutarasungnik, Eva Aruak	1926	E1-502	AR-99, W	1
Arviat	Okatsiak, Maxime	1941	E1-228	AR-57, H	1
Arviat	Okutak, Mathew	1937	E1-098	AR-23, H	1
Arviat	Ollie, John	1920	E1-139	AR-34, H	1
Arviat	Ootnooyuk, Susan	1918-1977	E1-285	AR-71, H (widow)	1
Arviat	Oruluk, Luke	1918-1978	E1-205	AR-51, H	1
Arviat	Oruluk, Martha Otunak	1921	E1-206	AR-51, W	9
Arviat	Oshutook, John	1920	E1-464	AR-92, H	5
Arviat	Otuk, Rosanna Nauyak	1931	E1-220	AR-54, W	1
Arviat	Otukpalanak, John	1910	E1-132	AR-32, H	3
Arviat	Otukpalanak, Rachael Ottuk	1915	E1-133	AR-32, W	2
Arviat	Owlijoot, Patsy	1955	E1-580	AR-37, A/D	3
Arviat	Pahuk, Melanie Tala	1934	E1-249	AR-72, W	2
Arviat	Pakimgnark				1
Arviat	Pameok, Madelain Katoo	1916	E1-284	AR-6, W	2
Arviat	Pangnark, John	1920-1980	E1-104	AR-25, H	45
Arviat	Panigoniak, Andrew	1947	E1-065	AR-7, A/S	1
Arviat	Sinnisiak, Andrew	1946	E1-036	AR-8, S	1
Arviat	Suluk, Bobby	1955	E1-594	AR-31, S	1
Arviat	Tagooguke, Murray	1942	E1-319	AR-76, H	1
Arviat	Tasseor Tutsweetok, Lucy	1934	E1-135	AR-70, W	33
Arviat	Tasseor, Nancy Kablutsiak	1935	E1-129	AR-33, W	4
Arviat	Tonowak, James Konerk	1931	E1-317	AR-75, H	14
Arviat	Tutsweetok, Richard	1929	E1-272	AR-70, H	1
Arviat	Ukutak, Susan Nibviak	1931-1988	E1-124	AR-39, W	1
Arviat	Ulayok, Vital	1948	E1-69		1
Arviat	Uppajuak, Judith Mainak	1937	E1-046	AR-37, W	3
Arviat	Utakajuak	1894-D	E1-062	AR-16, H	2
Arviat	Uvingayak, Issac	1928-1966	E1-189		7
Arviat	Uyauperq Aniksak, Margaret	1905-1993	E1-027	AR-7, W	7
Baker Lake	Aasivaaryuk, Peter	1914	E2-485	BL-85, H/D	3
Baker Lake	Agluvak, Marjorie	1921	E2-084	BL-71, W	1
Baker Lake	Akilak, Hattie	1938	E2-235	BL-57, W	1
Baker Lake	Akilak, Moses	1932	E2-254	BL-57, H	1
Baker Lake	Amarook, Michael	1941-1998	E2-275	BL-61, H	2
Baker Lake	Anautalik, Martha Tiktaq	1928-1995	E1-363	BL-88, W	1
Baker Lake	Anautalik, William	1931-1987	E1-362	BL-88, H	1
Baker Lake	Angnataratuk, Noah	1900-D	E3-031	BL-92, H	1
Baker Lake	Anguhadluq, Luke	1895-1982	E2-294	BL-63, H	5
Baker Lake	Aptanik, Martha	1915-1972	E2-224	BL-33, W	1
Baker Lake	Aqigaaq, Mathew	1940	E2-350	BL-71, H	2
Baker Lake	Arnakyuinaq, Paul	1926-1990	E2-178	BL-40, H	3
Baker Lake	Arnasungaaq, Barnabus	1924	E2-213	BL-47, H	13
Baker Lake	Arngna'naaq, Luke	1931-2000	E2-365	BL-74, H	5
Baker Lake	Arngna'naaq, Ruby	1947	E2-373	BL-74, S/D	1
Baker Lake	Arviktalik, Marie	1903-1975	E1-382	BL-89 H (widow)	1
Baker Lake	Aupaluktuq, Thomas Kalluk	1949	E2-438	BL-10, S	1
Baker Lake	Avaalaqiaq Tiktaalaaq, Irene	1941	E2-423	BL-22, W	1
Baker Lake	Ekalun, Patrick	1905-D	W2-19		2
Baker Lake	Eyetoaq, Ada	1934	E2-352	BL-50, W	3
Baker Lake	Ikinilik, Jacob	1934	E2-443	BL-82, H	1
Baker Lake	Ikuutaq, David	1929-1984	E2-349	BL-70, H	21
Baker Lake	Ikuutaq, Janet Nipi	1935	E2-234	BL-70, W	4
Baker Lake	Iqulik, Toona	1935	E2-167	BL-70,Br;Rl-14,H	12
Baker Lake	Kaluraq, Francis	1931-1990	E2-028	BL-8, H	3
Baker Lake	Kaluraq, Irene Taviniq	1934	E2-227	BL-8, W	2
Baker Lake	Kayuryuk, Samson	1927-1983	E2-065	BL-16, H	7
Baker Lake	Kigusiuq, Hannah	1931-1991	E2-173	BL-38, W	1
Baker Lake	Killulark, John	1935	E2-112	BL-27, H	2
Baker Lake	Kingak, James	1925-1990s	E2-107	BL-25, H	2
Baker Lake	Kingak, Madge	1922-1989	E2-086	BL-25, W	2
Baker Lake	Kingilik, Dominic	1939-1990	E2-121	BL-29, H	11
Baker Lake	Kingilik, James	1912-1970	E2-229	BL-50, H	2
Baker Lake	Kukiiyaut, Myra	1929	E2-210	BL-74, W	1
Baker Lake	Kuunnuaq, Marie	1933-1990	E2-126	BL-52, W	1
Baker Lake	Makpaaq, Vital	1922-1978	E2-120	BL-28, H	10
Baker Lake	Nagyugalik, Moses	1910-1995	E2-153	BL-35, H	1
Baker Lake	Niuqtuq, Eric	1937-1996	E2-181	BL-42, H	12
Baker Lake	Nuilaalik, Josiah	1928	E2-385	BL-75, H	8
Baker Lake	Nukik, John Haa'naaq	1935	E2-077	BL-20, H	1
Baker Lake	Ookaulleeyak, Moses	1925-1969	E2-132	BL-32, H	2
Baker Lake	Oovayuk, Thomas	1938	E2-129	BL-31, Bach.	1
Baker Lake	Owingayak, David	1941-1991	E3-034	BL-93, H	2
Baker Lake	Paungrat, Elizabeth	1938	E2-396	BL-55, W	1
Baker Lake	Qasariniq, Johnny	1902-1978	E2-344	BL-69, H	1
Baker Lake	Qaulluaryuk, Ruth	1932	E2-296	BL-75, W	2
Baker Lake	Qiyuk, Miriam	1933	E2-387	BL-77, W	2
Baker Lake	Qiyuk, Silas	1933	E2-397	BL-77, H	4
Baker Lake	Singaqti, Norman	1938	E2-299	BL-64, H	1
Baker Lake	Sivuraq, Thomas	1941	E2-236	BL-33, A/S	5
Baker Lake	Tapatai, John	1948	E2-408	BL-98, S	4
Baker Lake	Tatanniq, George	1910-1991	E2-179	BL-41, H	20
Baker Lake	Tiktaalaaq, David	1927-1999	E2-083	BL-22, H	2
Baker Lake	Tiriganiak, Hugh	1942-1971	E2-024	BL-6, S	1
Baker Lake	Toolooktook, Paul	1947	E2-377	BL-33, S/S	6
Baker Lake	Tuluqtuq, Julie	1935	E2-193	BL-51, W	1
Baker Lake	Tunguaq, Luke	1927	E2-192	BL-44, H	2
Baker Lake	Tunnuq, Elizabeth	1928	E2-133	BL-32, W	1
Baker Lake	Ukpatiku, William	1935	E2-363	BL-72, H	5
Baker Lake	Yuusipik Singaqti, Mary	1936	E2-388	BL-64, W	2
Bathurst Inlet	Damagso				1
Cape Dorset	Adla, Kalai	1927	E7-963	CD-31, H	1
Cape Dorset	Ashoona, Kaka	1928-1996	E7-1101	CD-65, H	6
Cape Dorset	Ashoona, Kiawak	1933	E7-1103	CD-67, H	4
Cape Dorset	Ashoona, Namoonai	1926	E7-1094	CD-63, H	1
Cape Dorset	Ashoona, Ottochie	1942-1970	E7-1105	CD-68, H	8
Cape Dorset	Etidlooie, Kingmeata	1915-1989	E7-895	CD-36, W	1
Cape Dorset	Etidlui, Etulu	1946	E7-989	CD-36, S	1
Cape Dorset	Igiu, Joanassie	1923-1981	E7-981	CD-35, H	2

Community	Artist's Name	Birth/Death	Disc Number	Family Number	# of Works	Community	Artist's Name	Birth/Death	Disc Number	Family Number	# of Works
Cape Dorset	Igiu, Mary	1925-1968	E7-982	CD-35, W	1	Cape Dorset	Tuqiqi, Koperqualuk	1944	E7-1110	CD-69, Br	1
Cape Dorset	Ipeelee, Osuitok	1923	E7-1154	CD-77, H	1	Chesterfield Inlet	Kimaliakyuk, Eli		E3-096	CI-10, H	1
Cape Dorset	Jaw, Melia	1934	E7-922	CD-40, W	1	Chesterfield Inlet	Qillaq, Donat	1914	E3-105	CI-24, H	2
Cape Dorset	Kellypalik, Mathew	1948	E7-769	CD-35, S	1	Chesterfield Inlet	Sammurtok, Isidore Tiktak	1930	E3-229	CI-29, H	4
Cape Dorset	Kingwatsiak, Iyola	1933-2000	E7-914	CD-23, H	1	Chesterfield Inlet	Sammurtok, Victor	1903-1980	E3-227	CI-28, H	1
Cape Dorset	Kingwatsiak, Mikigak	1943	E7-917	CD-24, H	5	Chesterfield Inlet	Unknown				1
Cape Dorset	Mangitak, Kellypalik	1940-1974	E7-999	CD-39, H	8	Clyde River	Iqalukjuak, Levi	1912-1988	E5-270		1
Cape Dorset	Mannumi, Davidee	1919-1979	E7-1063	CD-58, H	4	Coral Harbour	Jar, Timothy	1934	E3-724	CH	1
Cape Dorset	Mikkigak, Ohotaq	1936	E7-1009	CD-42, H	1	Coral Harbour	Nakoolak, Peecee	1947	E3-727	CH	1
Cape Dorset	Mikkigak, Qaunaq	1932	E7-1014	CD-42, W	1	Coral Harbour	Saimut, Joseph	1913-1969	E3-722	CH	3
Cape Dorset	Niviaksiak	1908-1959	E7-1077	CD-59?	1	Hall Beach	Kukkik, James	1949	E5-670	HB	1
Cape Dorset	Niviaqsi, Pitseolak	1947	E7-1081	CD-59, nephew	1	Igloolik	Iyerak, Alain	1920	E5-473		1
Cape Dorset	Nuna, Sharky	1918-1979	E7-883	CD-20, H	1	Inukjuak	Aculiak, Joe Adlaka	1936	E9-1595	In-54, S	2
Cape Dorset	Nungusuituq, Elisapee	1927	E7-1145	CD-73, W	3	Inukjuak	Aculiak, Josephie	1910-1968	E9-1593	In-54, H	11
Cape Dorset	Oshuitoq, Peesee	1913-1979	E7-932	CD-27, H	1	Inukjuak	Amidlak, Levi	1931	E9-1564	In-45, H	5
Cape Dorset	Ottokie, Johnny	1944	E7-1020	CD-46, a/s	1	Inukjuak	Amidlak, Mathewsie	1934	E9-1548	In-40, H	3
Cape Dorset	Parr, Epirvik	1946	E7-1027	CD-47, S	1	Inukjuak	Amidlak, Samwillie	1902-1984	E9-1546	In-39, H	1
Cape Dorset	Parr, Nuna	1949	E7-764	CD-47, S	2	Inukjuak	Annie				1
Cape Dorset	Pee, Aoudla	1920	E7-1043	CD-54, H	4	Inukjuak	Arnamissak, Jimmy Inaruli	1946	E9-962	PV-32, B	1
Cape Dorset	Pee, Etirayaqyuaq	1922	E7-947	CD-28, H	1	Inukjuak	Echalook, Aibilie	1940	E9-1647	In-64, H	1
Cape Dorset	Pee, Nuluapik	1919	E7-1044	CD-54, W	1	Inukjuak	Echalook, Jacob	1930-1965	E9-1644	In-63, H	1
Cape Dorset	Petaulassie, Aggeak	1922	E7-815	CD-11, H	2	Inukjuak	Echalook, Lucassie	1904	E9-1582	In-51, H	1
Cape Dorset	Petaulassie, Etidlui	1944	E7-817	CD-11, S	1	Inukjuak	Echalook, Moses	1931	E9-1585	In-52, H	2
Cape Dorset	Peter, Eyeetsiak	1937	E7-1150	CD-75, H	2	Inukjuak	Echalook, Noah	1946	E9-867	In-20, S	2
Cape Dorset	Pitseolak, Peter	1902-1973	E7-970	CD-32, H	2	Inukjuak	Echalook, Peter	1943	E9-1587	In-51, S	1
Cape Dorset	Pitsiulak, Ookpik	1948	E7-251	CD-4, D	1	Inukjuak	Echalook, Thomasee	1935	E9-1586	In-51, S	1
Cape Dorset	Pootoogook	1887-1958	E7-1166		1	Inukjuak	Elijassiapik, Harry	1943	E9-918	In-27, S	1
Cape Dorset	Pootoogook, Eegyvudluk	1931	E7-865	CD-16, H	1	Inukjuak	Epoo, Charlie	1913-1985	E9-1616	In-59, H	4
Cape Dorset	Pootoogook, Ishuhungitok	1939	E7-1062	CD-81, W	5	Inukjuak	Epoo, Johnny	1938	E9-1614	In-58, H	6
Cape Dorset	Pootoogook, Kananginak	1935	E7-1168	CD-78, H	1	Inukjuak	Inukpuk, Adamie	1943	E9-907	In-24, S	1
Cape Dorset	Pootoogook, Tookikalook	1943	E7-1178	CD-81, S	3	Inukjuak	Inukpuk, Charlie	1941	E9-906	In-25, H	1
Cape Dorset	Pudlat, Kanakpellik	1920-1965	E7-1082	CD-60, H(widow)	1	Inukjuak	Inukpuk, Daniel	1942	E9-882	In-21, S	1
Cape Dorset	Pudlat, Ningeoseak	1937	E7-872	CD-18, H	6	Inukjuak	Kasudluak, Allie	1926-1982	E9-1670	In-67, H	1
Cape Dorset	Pudlat, Simeonie	1943	E7-1000	CD-36, S	2	Inukjuak	Kasudluak, Daniel	1925	E9-1699	In-70, H	1
Cape Dorset	Qayuaryuk, Anashuk	1940	E7-1071	CD-44, W	1	Inukjuak	Kasudluak, Davidee	1913	E9-1552	In-41, H	1
Cape Dorset	Qayuaryuk, Laisa	1935	E7-1015	CD-44, H	1	Inukjuak	Kasudluak, Isa	1917-1997	E9-1701	In-71, H	3
Cape Dorset	Qayuaryuk, Mary	1908-1982	E7-1012	CD-43, W	2	Inukjuak	Kasudluak, Jamasie	1935	E9-1666	In-67, B	3
Cape Dorset	Qimirpik, Kellypalik	1948	E7-754	CD-A, H	5	Inukjuak	Kasudluak, Johnnie	1944	E9-780	In-14, S	1
Cape Dorset	Qinnuayuak, Tikituk	1908	E7-1067	CD-59, H	5	Inukjuak	Kasudluak, Paulosie	1938	E9-779	In-15, H	2
Cape Dorset	Quppapik, Simeonie	1909	E7-868	CD-17, H	1	Inukjuak	Kasudluak, Paulosie	1928	E9-1717	In-77, B	3
Cape Dorset	Ragee, Kuppapik	1931	E7-837	CD-13, H	1	Inukjuak	Kasudluak, Peter	1906-1982	E9-777	In-14, H	5
Cape Dorset	Saggiak	1897-1980	E7-1190	CD-82, H	3	Inukjuak	Kasudluak, Simon	1925	E9-1716	In-77, H	1
Cape Dorset	Saggiak, Kumakuluk	1944	E7-1192	CD-82, S	4	Inukjuak	Kingalik, Samson	1937	E9-712	In-5, H	1
Cape Dorset	Sagiatuk, Sagiatuk	1932	E7-716	CD-9, H	1	Inukjuak	Kingalik, Simeonie	1930	E9-710	In-4, H	1
Cape Dorset	Saila, Pauta	1916	E7-990	CD-37, H	12	Inukjuak	Kumarluk, Lucassie	1921	E9-704	In-2, H	2
Cape Dorset	Samualie, Johnny Toon	1940	E7-953	CD-29, S/S	3	Inukjuak	Kutchaka, Timothy	1924	E9-774	In-13, H	11
Cape Dorset	Shaa, Aqjangajuk	1937	E7-1065	CD-58, S	1	Inukjuak	Nalukturuk, Josephie	1936	E9-1735	In-78, H	1
Cape Dorset	Simeonie, Simigak	1939	E7-868	CD-17, H	3	Inukjuak	Nalukturuk, Simeonie	1953	E9-2113	In-78, S	1
Cape Dorset	Takpaungai, Quvianatuliak	1942	E7-1093	CD-61, S	1	Inukjuak	Nastapoka, Abraham	1900-1981	E9-1706	In-74, H	5
Cape Dorset	Teevee, Jamasie	1910-1985	E7-977	CD-34, H	2	Inukjuak	Nastapoka, Davidee	1945	E9-1708	In-74, S	1
Cape Dorset	Tooloogak, Pauloosie	1925-1991	E1-417	AR-?	3	Inukjuak	Nastapoka, Samson	1931	E9-1712	In-76, H	3
Cape Dorset	Toonoo	1920-1969	E7-1111	CD-69, H	2	Inukjuak	Nastapoka, Sarah	1925	E9-1519	In-74, W	2
Cape Dorset	Tuckyashuk	1898-1972	E7-1028	CD-51, H	1	Inukjuak	Nayoumealook, Conlucy	1940-1966	E9-1572	In-48, H	6
Cape Dorset	Tudlik	1890-1966	E7-1050	CD-56, father	2	Inukjuak	Nayoumealook, Timothy	1943	E9-1573	In-47, S	3

Community	Artist's Name	Birth/ Death	Disc Number	Family Number	# of Works	Community	Artist's Name	Birth/ Death	Disc Number	Family Number	# of Works
Inukjuak	Niviaxie, Adamie	1925	E9-731	In-7, H	6	Kimmirut	Ohaituk, Simeonie	1941	E9-924		1
Inukjuak	Niviaxie, Conlucy	1892-D	E9-728	In-8, F	3	Kimmirut	Padluq, Eliyah	1941	E7-175		1
Inukjuak	Niviaxie, Jeremiah	1942	E9-736	In-8, Br	2	Kimmirut	Padluq, Josephie	1931	E7-679		2
Inukjuak	Nowkawalk, Joanasie	1926	E9-908	In-26, H	2	Kimmirut	Padluq, Pauloosie	1917-1983	E7-172		7
Inukjuak	Nowra, Johnnie	1948	E9-1806	In-23, S	1	Kimmirut	Pitsiulak, George	1929	E7-41		2
Inukjuak	Nowra, Peter	1929	E9-890	In-20, B	1	Kimmirut	Qayuaryuk, Joanassie	1928	E7-907		3
Inukjuak	Nowrakudluk, Lucassie	1912-1981	E9-1620	In-62, H	3	Kimmirut	Qimirpik, Nuyaliaq	1937	E7-99		6
Inukjuak	Nowrakudluk, Mary	1932	E9-1730	In-56, W	1	Kimmirut	Temela, Agee	1912	E7-66		1
Inukjuak	Nowrakudluk, Noah	1916	E9-1612	In-56, H	1	Kimmirut	Tikivik, Oomagajuk	1921	E7-243		1
Inukjuak	Nulukie, Josie	1931-1980	E9-1660	In-65, S	1	Kugaaruk	Makittuq, Lea Aarlu	1940	E4-317		2
Inukjuak	Owgeak, Isaac	1934	E9-768	In-12, A/S	1	Kugaaruk	Qirngnuq, Helene Qarqmatsiaq	1913	E4-518		1
Inukjuak	Paulosie, Noah Tukai	1938	E9-1542	In-38, S	1	Kuujjuaraapik	Alayco, Issac	1941	E9-1737		3
Inukjuak	Paulosie, Paulosie	1915-1979	E9-1540	In-38, H	1	Kuujjuaraapik	Alayco, Lucassie	1942	E9-1069		1
Inukjuak	Pov, Abraham	1927	E9-884	In-23, H	2	Kuujjuaraapik	Alayko, Solomonie	1906	E9-1066		1
Inukjuak	Pov, Moses	1915	E9-791	In-16, H	1	Kuujjuaraapik	Angutiguluk, Daniel	1908-1980	E9-222	GWR	1
Inukjuak	Qinuajua, Sarah Joe	1917-1986	E9-823	Puv-10, W	2	Kuujjuaraapik	Annieoole				1
Inukjuak	Qumaluk, Elizabeth	1927	E9-842		1	Kuujjuaraapik	Aragutak, Alice	1922	E9-1784		1
Inukjuak	Simaotik, Daniel	1907-1968	E9-1592	In-53, H	1	Kuujjuaraapik	Cookie, Mary	1934	E9-261		1
Inukjuak	Smiler, Aisa	1921-1986	E9-706	In-3, H	3	Kuujjuaraapik	Niviaxie, Annie	1930-1989	E9-1720		3
Inukjuak	Tuki, Joe Adamie	1943	E9-931	In-28, S	4	Kuujjuaraapik	Niviaxie, Silassie	1934	E9-732	In-8, H	3
Inukjuak	Tuki, Lucassie	1935	E9-1773	In-83, S	2	Kuujjuaraapik	Papialuk, Adamie	1919	E9-1047		1
Inukjuak	Tuki, Sima	1911-1967	E9-927	In-28, H	2	Kuujjuaraapik	Sala, Gina	1903-1988	E9-1719		2
Inukjuak	Weetaluktuk, Simeonie	1910	E9-1752	In-81, H	1	Kuujjuaraapik	Sala, Samson	1931	E9-1724		1
Inukjuak	Weetaluktuk, Syollie	1906-1962	E9-1745	In-79, H	2	Kuujjuaraapik	Sappa, Davidee	1930	E9-325		3
Iqaluit	Annahatuk, Emily	1919	E8-647		2	Kuujjuaraapik	Tooktoo, Willie	1933	E9-362		1
Iqaluit	Ennutsiak	1896-1967			1	Kuujjuaraapik	Tuktu, Charlie	1926	E9-361		1
Iqaluit	Evaluardjuk, Henry	1923	E5-846		1	Kuujjuaraapik	Weetaltuk, John	1939			1
Iqaluit	Manno	1923-1973	E7-887		1	Pangnirtung	Akpalialuk, Jacob	1947	E6-525		2
Iqaluit	Ningeoak, Davidee	1925-1988	E9-762		2	Pangnirtung	Akulukjuk, Joshua	1939	E6-398		1
Iqaluit	Ningeoseak, Peter	1937	E7-1137		1	Pangnirtung	Kakkik, Joanasee	1919-1998	F6-45		2
Iqaluit	Nuna, Noah	1900	E7-877		1	Pangnirtung	Karpik, Pauloosie	1911-1988	E6-187		2
Iqaluit	Pitsiulaq, Peter	1911	E5-614	Igloolik	1	Pangnirtung	Kilabuk, Jim Natsiapik	1902-1984	E6-18		1
Iqaluit	Shuvigar, Eelee	1904-1977	E7-939		1	Pangnirtung	Maniapik, Manasee	1939	E6-290		1
Ivujivik	Iyaituk, Markusi	1906	E9-963	IV-23, H	2	Pangnirtung	Naulalik, Solomon	1929	E6-280		1
Ivujivik	Luuku, Saima Qaunnaaluk	1930	E9-976	IV-02, S	2	Pangnirtung	Nowyook, Nicodemus	1902-1985	E6-376		1
Ivujivik	Nauja, Juanisi	1927-1965	E9-975	IV-21, H	2	Pangnirtung	Nuvaqirq, Josephee	1947	E6-534		1
Ivujivik	Nauya, Lizzie Aviliajuk	1930	E9-1024	IV-21, W	1	Pangnirtung	Pitsiulak, Lipa	1943	E6-436		1
Ivujivik	Qaunnaaluk, Paulusi	1927	E9-1062	IV-05, H	1	Pangnirtung	Pitsiulak, Markosee Joan	1895-1980	E6-355		1
Kangiqsualujjuaq	Annanack, Johnny George	1926	E8-503		1	Pond Inlet	Pitseolak, Seeana	1938	E5-695		1
Kangiqsualujjuaq	Baron, Christina	1942	E8-565		1	Puvirnituq	Amamartua, Adamie Suppaki	1930	E9-944	Puv-25, H	1
Kangiqsualujjuaq	Emuk, Elsie	1901-1983	E8-650		1	Puvirnituq	Amamartua, Lukasi Ananagi	1935	E9-945	Puv-26, H	1
Kangirsuk	Anitook				1	Puvirnituq	Amaruali, Matiusi Ilimasaut	1931	E9-804	Puv-4, H	2
Kangirsuk	Eetook, Josephie	1913	E8-822		1	Puvirnituq	Amittu, Davidialuk Alasua	1910-1976	E9-824	Puv-11, H	9
Kangirsuk	Kudluk, Thomassie	1910-1989	E8-873		1	Puvirnituq	Amittu, Minnie Angutausugi	1930	E9-828	Puv-6, W	1
Kangirsuk	Lucassie, Lucassie	1911	E8-864		1	Puvirnituq	Anauta, Makusi Pangutu	1939	E9-1354	Puv-44, S	4
Kangirsuk	Nassak, Sammy	1905-1988	E8-899		1	Puvirnituq	Angiju, Daniel Quma	1929-1979	E9-952	In-31, H	1
Kimmirut	Akavak, Moosa	1949	E7-290		4	Puvirnituq	Angutikirq, Peter Iqallu	1919	E9-1487	Puv-78, H	1
Kimmirut	Annawak, Anuraq	1894-1988	E7-21		2	Puvirnituq	Assappa, Maina Aqurtu	1909	E9-825	Puv-11, W	1
Kimmirut	Arlooktoo, Joe	1939	E7-17		3	Puvirnituq	Assappa, Timothy Qiatalla	1914-1982	E9-811	Puv-6, H	1
Kimmirut	Kolola, Mosesie	1930-1985	E7-231		2	Puvirnituq	Augia, Tumasi Illuta	1912	E9-1347	Puv-43, H	1
Kimmirut	Koughajuke, Noah	1899-1976	E7-210		2	Puvirnituq	Aupalu, Paulusi Passau	1918	E9-1301	Puv-33, H	1
Kimmirut	Kowjakoolook, Simeonie	1906-1985	E7-86		2	Puvirnituq	Aupaluk, Joanassie	1925-1963	E9-1379	Puv-52, H	3
Kimmirut	Lookak, Liote	unknown			1	Puvirnituq	Aupaluktuk, Moses	1924-1983	E9-833		1
Kimmirut	Lyta, Joanasie	1921	E7-238		1	Puvirnituq	Igauja, Aisapik Quma	1915-1979	E9-1484	Puv-70,Br-in-law	22

Community	Artist's Name	Birth/Death	Disc Number	Family Number	# of Works
Puvirnituq	Ijikitu, Sarah Tillikasa	1928-1988	E9-770	Puv-12, W	1
Puvirnituq	Ivilla, Samisa Passauralu	1924	E9-806	Puv-5, H	12
Puvirnituq	Johmahl, Johniahl		E9-1458	Puv-?	1
Puvirnituq	Kuanana, Caroline Talitu	1925-1992	E9-1451	In-35, W	1
Puvirnituq	Kuanana, Daniel Nuluki	1936	E9-1444	Puv-66, H	1
Puvirnituq	Kuanana, Makusi Nunga	1932	E9-1443	Puv-65, H	2
Puvirnituq	Kuanana, Timothy Kuananapik	1938-1984	E9-1445	Puv-64, S	1
Puvirnituq	Luuku, Mattiusi Qimmialuk	1936	E9-977	Puv-?	2
Puvirnituq	Napatu, Eliassiapik Aullalu	1913-1966	E9-1384	Puv-54, H	1
Puvirnituq	Nutaraalu, Echaluk	1941	E9-1392	Puv-55, S	1
Puvirnituq	Papialuk, Isah	1926	E9-1413	Puv-58, H	2
Puvirnituq	Papialuk, Josie Pamiutu	1918-1997	E9-861		1
Puvirnituq	Putugu, Johnny Tukala	1943	E9-1416	Puv-59, H	1
Puvirnituq	Qauritaiju, Pitajusi Uriju	1905	E9-1327	Puv-38, A/Br	1
Puvirnituq	Qiluqi, Matiusi Manukullu	1911-1968	E9-1314	Puv-35, H	2
Puvirnituq	Qinuajua, Eli Sallualu	1937	E9-846	Puv-18, S	2
Puvirnituq	Qinuajua, Noah	1913-1962	E9-822	Puv-10, H	1
Puvirnituq	Quananak, Pauloosie	1899-1963	E9-1441	Puv-64, H	3
Puvirnituq	Qumalu, Eli Umajualu	1940	E9-841	Puv-14, S	1
Puvirnituq	Qumalu, Mary Luisa Pualu	1932	E9-838	Puv-8, W	1
Puvirnituq	Qumaluk, Jusi	1929-1984	E9-837	Puv-15, H	3
Puvirnituq	Sivuak, Paulosie	1930-1986	E9-1493	Puv-?	1
Puvirnituq	Sivuaraapik, Charlie	1911-1968	E9-1460	Puv-70, H	2
Puvirnituq	Sivuarapik, Simiuni	1946	E9-1463	Puv-70, S	1
Puvirnituq	Smith, Isapik	1931-1970	E9-1331	Puv-39, A/S	4
Puvirnituq	Smith, Levi Alasua Pirti	1927-1986	E9-1326	Puv-38, H	1
Puvirnituq	Talirunili, Joe	1906-1976	E9-818	Puv-9, H	2
Puvirnituq	Tukala, Aisara Ajagutaina	1942	E9-1440	Puv-63, S	1
Puvirnituq	Tukalak, Aisa Ajagutainnaq	1905-1977	E9-1432	Puv-62, H	1
Puvirnituq	Tukalak, Qumaluk	1936	E9-1438	Puv-59, S	1
Puvirnituq	Tullaugu, David Alasua	1941	E9-1339	Puv-40, S	1
Puvirnituq	Tuluga, Aisa	1899-1971	E9-853	Puv-21, F	2
Puvirnituq	Uqaitu, Juaniapi Angutigulu	1937	E9-1456	Puv-69, S	1
Rankin Inlet	Ahkanayo				1
Rankin Inlet	Aiyarani, Sevoui	1916-1988	E3-010	RI-24, H	1
Rankin Inlet	Aksadjuak, Laurent	1935-2002	E1-017	RI-1, H	2
Rankin Inlet	Alikasuak, Eve Kudluk	1923	E1-480	RI-8, W	7
Rankin Inlet	Angatajuak, Joseph	1935-1976	E1-486	RI-11, H	7
Rankin Inlet	Angutituak, Michael	1912	W1-231	RI-96, H	1
Rankin Inlet	Ayaruak, John	1907-1988	E3-054	RI-30, H	1
Rankin Inlet	Ayaruak, John Kaudyadyuk	1950	E3-1015	RI-30, S	1
Rankin Inlet	Ikkuti, Nicholas	1920-D	E1-390	RI-6, H	1
Rankin Inlet	Iyakak, Edward	1928	E3-540	RI-81, H	1
Rankin Inlet	Kabluitok, Eugenie Tautoonie	1914-1986	E3-086	RI-37, W	6
Rankin Inlet	Kabluitok, Jacques	1912-1973	E3-085	RI-37, H	1
Rankin Inlet	Kabluitok, Lucien Tootuk	1949	E3-596	RI-37, S	1
Rankin Inlet	Kavik, John	1897-1993	E2-290	RI-16, H	10
Rankin Inlet	Kolit, Simon	1917	E3-121	RI-41, H	1
Rankin Inlet	Kowtak, Andy	1942	E1-482	RI-10, H	1
Rankin Inlet	Kukshout, Pie	1911-1980	E2-302	RI-96 (boarder)	4
Rankin Inlet	Manernaluk, Anthony	1931	W1-207	RI-95, H	1
Rankin Inlet	Nauya, Pierre	1914-1977	E3-174	RI-52, H	1
Rankin Inlet	Okalik, John	1925	E1-349	RI-5, H	1
Rankin Inlet	Okoktok, Pierre	1949	E3-1001	RI-58, S	1

Community	Artist's Name	Birth/Death	Disc Number	Family Number	# of Works
Rankin Inlet	Okoktok, Vital	1912	E3-204	RI-58, H	3
Rankin Inlet	Oshutook, Elizabeth Nanuq	1910	E1-465		1
Rankin Inlet	Paniguniark, Charles	1946	E3-013	RI-26, H	1
Rankin Inlet	Piola, Tana Sanayaga				1
Rankin Inlet	Snoo				1
Rankin Inlet	Tikeayak, Eli	1933	E2-166	RI-13, S	11
Rankin Inlet	Tiktak, John	1916-1981	E1-266	RI-4, H	17
Rankin Inlet	Tiktak, Thomas	1950	E1-513	RI-4, S	1
Rankin Inlet	Ugjuk, Thomas	1921	E2-288	RI-15, H	3
Rankin Inlet	Ukutak, David	1927	E1-154	AR-39, H	1
Repulse Bay	Aglukka, Honore	1943	E3-494	RB-17, H	1
Repulse Bay	Airut, Eva		E3-403		1
Repulse Bay	Airut, Katherine Karjenayok	1948	E3-525	RB-4, D	1
Repulse Bay	Ajotieak				1
Repulse Bay	Akkuardjuk, Lucie Eeyaitok	1921	E5-625	RB-29, W	25
Repulse Bay	Akkuardjuk, Paul	1914-1974	E3-578	RB-29, H	16
Repulse Bay	Angotingoar, Elizabeth Uluta	1948	E3-854	RB-7, W	9
Repulse Bay	Angotingoar, Lionel	1905	E3-422		1
Repulse Bay	Angotingoar, Olalie Olartituk	1916	E3-772		5
Repulse Bay	Anguitok, Anthanese	1911	E3-456	RB-11, H	11
Repulse Bay	Angutialuk, Cecilia Angmadlok	1938	E3-482	RB-15, Widow?	7
Repulse Bay	Angutialuk, Tingmi		E3-545		7
Repulse Bay	Angutitaq, Irene Katak	1914-1971	E3-457	RB-11, W	66
Repulse Bay	Angutitok, Athanese	1911	E3-456		1
Repulse Bay	Antosh				1
Repulse Bay	Arnadluar, Joseph	1946	E3-507	RB-27, A/Son	1
Repulse Bay	Aupillardjuk, Mariano	1923	E3-407	RB-4, H	30
Repulse Bay	Aupillardjuk, Marie Tullimar	1927	E3-408	RB-4, W	30
Repulse Bay	Crawford, Agatha	1947	E3-548	RB-5, D	1
Repulse Bay	Irniq, Peter	1941	E3-546	RB-11, S	1
Repulse Bay	Inerdjuk, John	1938	E5-87	AB-11, H (widow)	5
Repulse Bay	Ivalooarjuk, Bernadette Saumik	1938	E3-539	RB-20, W	75
Repulse Bay	Kanatsiak, Jimmy	1945	E3-905	RB-35, H	2
Repulse Bay	Kanayok, Pierre	1908	E3-431	RB-8, H	1
Repulse Bay	Kanayok, Rosa Arnarudluk	1914-1984	E3-480	RB-6, W	20
Repulse Bay	Katokra, Marguerite Anernerk	1934	E5-527	RB-3, W	10
Repulse Bay	Katokra, Peter	1931	E3-358	RB-3, H	23
Repulse Bay	Kaunak, Felicite Kuwianartok	1924	E3-195	RB-24, W	21
Repulse Bay	Kaunak, Gabriel	1952	E3-1037	RB-24, S/Son	2
Repulse Bay	Kaunak, John	1941	E3-520	RB-24, H	88
Repulse Bay	Keelawajuk, Philuardjuk	1901-1988	E7-967		8
Repulse Bay	Kidlapik, Sata Jamesie	1945	E7-969	RB-42, H	4
Repulse Bay	Kileekuk, Kilahuh				1
Repulse Bay	Kipanik, David Nuluk	1952-1988	E3-931	RB-38, H	5
Repulse Bay	Kipanik, Najuga	1923-1988	E3-518		5
Repulse Bay	Kitiark				1
Repulse Bay	Kopak, Rosalie Ookangok	1935-2000	E3-463		1
Repulse Bay	Kridluar, Marius	1949	E3-532	RB-25, H	10
Repulse Bay	Kringayark, Madeleine Isserkut	1928-1986	E3-411	RB-5, W	63
Repulse Bay	Kringayark, Nicholas	1921	E3-410	RB-5, H	20
Repulse Bay	Kringayark, Simona	1953	E3-945	RB-5, D	8
Repulse Bay	Mablik, Anthonese	1940	E3-581	RB-31, H	32
Repulse Bay	Mablik, Suzanne Tupitnerk	1942	E3-500	RB-31, W	47
Repulse Bay	Manilak, Cajetan	1934	E3-503	RI-78, H	7

Community	Artist's Name	Birth/Death	Disc Number	Family Number	# of Works
Repulse Bay	Manilak, Veronica Kadjuak	1935	E3-450		3
Repulse Bay	Manitok, Paul	1947	E3-671	RB-14, Br	2
Repulse Bay	Mapsalak, Jean	1930	E3-476	RB-13, H	4
Repulse Bay	Mapsalak, Lucie Angalakte	1931	E3-481	RB-13, W	20
Repulse Bay	Mapsalak, Maria	1950	E3-918	RB-13, S/D	19
Repulse Bay	Mary				2
Repulse Bay	Milortok, Martha Ulliyak	1944	E3-412	RB-5, D	21
Repulse Bay	Nanorak, Alice Utakralak	1939	E3-487	RB-33, W	9
Repulse Bay	Nanorak, Francois	1946	E3-583	RB-33, H	9
Repulse Bay	Nanordluk, AlezinaNatar Panana	1943	E3-478	RB-18, W	32
Repulse Bay	Nanordluk, Jaki	1937	E3-499	RB-18, H	9
Repulse Bay	Nobvak, Apollina	1906-1965	E3-502	RB-27,Mother	76
Repulse Bay	Noyarth				1
Repulse Bay	Oksokitok, Agnes Aulak	1927-1988	E3-417	RB-6, W (deceased?)	1
Repulse Bay	Oksokitok, Jean Ivalutannar	1944	E3-418	RB-7, H	5
Repulse Bay	Oksokitok, Louis	1926	E3-416	RB-6, H	24
Repulse Bay	Paniuq, Natuq Quliktalik	1948	E3-382		3
Repulse Bay	Pudjat, Lea Arnauyark	1900	E3-512	RB-22, H (Widow)	17
Repulse Bay	Putulik, Arsene Pangakra	1935	E3-580	RB-30, H	4
Repulse Bay	Putulik, Celina Seeleenak	1934	E3-491	RB-30, W	61
Repulse Bay	Qanatsiaq, Letia Nattuk	1947	E5-561		3
Repulse Bay	Qattalik, Martha	1948	E3-906		2
Repulse Bay	Sarpisiuk		E3-551		3
Repulse Bay	Satuqsi, Theophile	1949	E3-531	RB-28, S	2
Repulse Bay	Saumik, Thomas	1942	E3-506	RB-20, H	6
Repulse Bay	Siatsak, Antoine	1945	E5-627	RB-29, S/Son	8
Repulse Bay	Siusangnark, Panniark	1934-1988	E3-515	RB-43, W	12
Repulse Bay	Siusangnark, Paul	1929-1980	E7-1085	RB-43, H	19
Repulse Bay	Siutinuar, Andreas	1947	E3-542	RB-6, S	7
Repulse Bay	Siutinuar, Annie Kopainuk	1948	E5-652	S/Dau	18
Repulse Bay	Sivanertok, Christine Aaluk	1938	E3-360	RB-27, W	87
Repulse Bay	Sivanertok, Nicholas	1948	E3-528	RB-27, A/Son	1
Repulse Bay	Sivanertok, Octave	1924	E3-547	RB-27, H	6
Repulse Bay	Tabo, Mathias Niuvitsiak	1947-1971	E3-508	RB-26, S	1
Repulse Bay	Tattuinee, Jerome	1932	E3-454	RB-5? Son-in-law	7
Repulse Bay	Teegonak, Abraham	1926	E3-513	RB-23, H	2
Repulse Bay	Teegonak, Letia Koonoo	1923	E3-909		14
Repulse Bay	Teegonak, Sakpinark	1948	E3-911		1
Repulse Bay	Theayak				1
Repulse Bay	Tigumiar, Philomen Kramukka	1943	E3-582	RB-32, H	29
Repulse Bay	Tinashlu, Charlie	1935	E3-477	RB-14, H	5
Repulse Bay	Tinashlu, John	1949	E3-533	RB-14, S/Son	4
Repulse Bay	Tinashlu, Johnasy	1948	E3-522	RB-14, S/Son	1
Repulse Bay	Tongelik, Bernadette Iguptark	1931-1984	E3-458	RB-36, W	74
Repulse Bay	Tongelik, Victor	1924	E3-912	RB-36, H	22
Repulse Bay	Tugumiar, Therese Paolak	1944	E5-560	RB-32, W	24
Repulse Bay	Tuktadjuk, Tuktudyu David	1946	E3-910	RB-23, S	3
Repulse Bay	Tungilik, Cecilia Arnadjuk	1938	E3-504	RB-34, W	16
Repulse Bay	Tungilik, Louise Anguatsiark	1917-1988	E5-442	RB-1,W	19
Repulse Bay	Tungilik, Mark	1913-1986	E3-320	RB-1, H	40
Repulse Bay	Ullikatar, Anthanese	1908-1972	E3-356	RB-2, H	66
Salluit	Angutigirk, Charlie Kalingoapik	1938	E9-1116		1
Salluit	Cliyul				1
Salluit	Ilisituk, Jeannie Tunu	1934	E9-1109		1
Salluit	Ilisituk, Padli Uttuujaq	1931	E9-1212		2
Salluit	Ilisituk, Tivi	1933	E9-1213		3
Salluit	July				1
Salluit	Kadyulik, Annie Kinnaujaq	1928	E9-1150		2
Salluit	Kadyulik, Joby Kudlu	1936	E9-1147		2
Salluit	Kaitak, Joanasi Kimatut	1921	E9-1091		2
Salluit	Keatainak, Eva Atammiq	1919	E9-1119		2
Salluit	Koperqualuk, Thomasie	1917	E9-1008		1
Salluit	Kumak, Mary Kiinalik	1923	E9-1131		1
Salluit	Kupirkrualuk, Audlaluk	1926	E9-1031		1
Salluit	Kupirkrualuk, Josepie Ningiok	1930	E9-1032		1
Salluit	Lola				1
Salluit	Naluiyuk, Joanasi	1917	E9-1155		1
Salluit	Naluiyuk, Kakinik	1946	E9-1157		1
Salluit	Okituk, Lily Uijakki	1933	E9-1012		1
Salluit	Okituk, Paulusi Quanak	1934-1972	E9-1190		2
Salluit	Padlayat, Isaaci Qurqaq	1934	E9-1161		1
Salluit	Qinuajua, Lukasi Kanarjua	1937	E9-1363		1
Salluit	Sakiagak, Eva Tukirqi	1946	E9-1172		1
Salluit	Sakiagak, Mathewsie	1923	E9-1201		2
Salluit	Saviakjuk, Ittukutaaq	1924	E9-1134		1
Salluit	Saviakjuk, Josepie Qupirqualuk	1935	E9-1137		2
Salluit	Sorusiluk, Mary Irqiquq	1897-1966	E9-1093		1
Salluit	Tarkirk, Jamie Qajuurtaq	1936	E9-1055		2
Salluit	Tayarak, George Kopak	1931	E9-1167		1
Salluit	Tayarak, Maggie Ittuvik	1898-1961	E9-1165		1
Salluit	Tayarak, Pialli	1919-1964	E7-269		1
Salluit	Yugalak, Adamie	1927	E9-1092		1
Salluit	Yuliasie, Nunivak	1918	E3-754		1
Sanikiluaq	Amitook, Isaac	1916	E9-1	San-1, H	13
Sanikiluaq	Appaqaq Jr., Allie	1943	E9-10	San-3, H	7
Sanikiluaq	Appaqaq, Allie	1915-1986	E9-8	San-2, H	4
Sanikiluaq	Appaqaq, Moses	1946	E9-156	San-28, H	12
Sanikiluaq	Emiqutailaq, George	1946	E9-88	San-18, S	1
Sanikiluaq	Emiqutailaq, Joe	1918	E9-85	San-18, H	4
Sanikiluaq	Emiqutailaq, Mina	1921	E9-86	San-18, W	1
Sanikiluaq	Eyaituq, Davidee	1935	E9-31	San-9, H	2
Sanikiluaq	Eyaituq, Johnassie	1944	E9-33	San-8, Br	3
Sanikiluaq	Eyaituq, Mina	1951	E9-195	San-1, D	3
Sanikiluaq	Eyaituq, Sophia	1943	E9-48	San-9, W	1
Sanikiluaq	Innuktaluk, Lucassie	1934	E9-150	San-27, H	1
Sanikiluaq	Ippak, Alec	1940	E9-36	San-11, S	9
Sanikiluaq	Ippak, Moses	1916	E9-34	San-11, H	5
Sanikiluaq	Iqaluq, Samwillie	1925	E9-19	San-5, H	3
Sanikiluaq	Kavik, Davidee	1915	E9-130	GWR	5
Sanikiluaq	Kavik, Elijassie	1947	E9-153	San-13, S	4
Sanikiluaq	Kavik, Johnassie	1916-1984	E9-56	San-13, H	11
Sanikiluaq	Kavik, Sarah	1924	E9-57	San-13, W	1
Sanikiluaq	Kudlurok, Charlie	1933	E9-1628	San-34, H	1
Sanikiluaq	Mannuk, Johnassie	1929	E9-24	San-7, H	6
Sanikiluaq	Meeko, Johnny	1933	E9-68	San-15, H	2
Sanikiluaq	Meeko, Moses	1920-1975	E9-22	San-6, H	6
Sanikiluaq	Meeko, Samson	1939	E9-32	San-10, H	1
Sanikiluaq	Naralik, Timothy	1942-1980	E9-73	San-16, H	5

Community	Artist's Name	Birth/Death	Disc Number	Family Number	# of Works
Sanikiluaq	Novalinga, Daniel	1928	E9-97	San-19, H	4
Sanikiluaq	Novalinga, Lucy	1936	E9-107	San-19, W	1
Sanikiluaq	Oqaituq, Annie	1947	E9-154	San-14, D	1
Sanikiluaq	Oqaituq, Lucassie	1921	E9-59	San-14, H	10
Sanikiluaq	Oqaituq, Noah	1949	E9-177	San-14, S	1
Sanikiluaq	Qittusuk, Annie	1940	E9-108	San-20, D	2
Sanikiluaq	Qittusuk, Caroline Onganguaq	1911-1979	E9-104	San-20, W	1
Sanikiluaq	Qittusuk, Charlie	1927	E9-109	San-21, H	12
Sanikiluaq	Qittusuk, Lucassie	1908-1978	E9-103	San-20, H	8
Sanikiluaq	Qittusuk, Sarah	1930	E9-110	San-21, W	1
Sanikiluaq	Takatak, Isaac	1930	E9-113	San-22, H	3
Sanikiluaq	Takatak, Lucassie	1942	E9-117	San-22, Br	6
Sanikiluaq	Tukallak, Johnassie	1912-1988	E9-121	San-23, H	6
Sanikiluaq	Tukallak, Johnny	1935	E9-124	San-23, S	3
Sanikiluaq	Tukallak, Silas	1950	E9-185	San-23, S	1
Sanikiluaq	Uppik, Simeonie	1928-1988	E9-84	San-17, H	2
Sanikiluaq	Iqaluq, Johnassie	1934	E9-18	San-4, H	1
Taloyoak	Adamie		E4-?	Tal	1
Taloyoak	Aqqaq, Stephen	1933	E4-511		1
Taloyoak	Ashevak, Karoo	1940-1974	E4-196		1
Whale Cove	Agjuk, John	1914	W1-236	WC-	1
Whale Cove	Aniksak, Neree	1906	E1-078	WC-7, H	1
Whale Cove	Aniksak, Sherktanak	1911	E1-079	WC-7, W	1

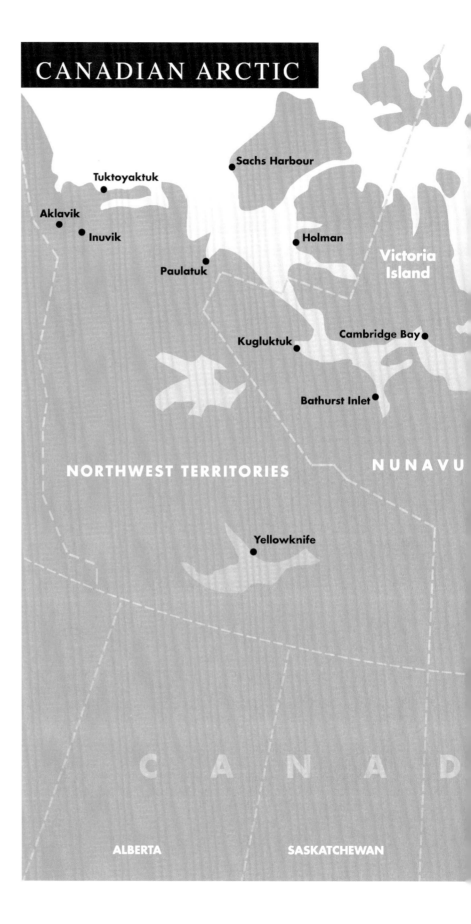

CANADIAN ARCTIC

Sachs Harbour

Tuktoyaktuk

Aklavik

Inuvik

Holman

Paulatuk

Victoria
Island

Cambridge Bay

Kugluktuk

Bathurst Inlet

NORTHWEST TERRITORIES

NUNAVU

Yellowknife

C A N A D

ALBERTA

SASKATCHEWAN

Grise Fiord

GREENLAND

lute

Nanisivik

Arctic Bay   Pond Inlet

Clyde River

Baffin Island

Qikiqtarjuaq

Igloolik

Taloyoak

Pangnirtung

Hall Beach

Gjoa Haven   Kugaaruk

Repulse Bay

Iqaluit

Cape Dorset

Kimmirut

Baker Lake   Coral Harbour

Kangiqsujuaq

Ivujivik

Chesterfield Inlet   Salluit   Quaqtaq

Kangiqsualujjuaq

Rankin Inlet

Akulivik   Kangirsuk

Nain

hale Cove

Puvirnituq   Kuujjuaq

Arviat

Makkovik

Rigolet

NUNAVIK

Hudson Bay

Inukjuak

Happy Valley - Goose Bay

Churchill

Umiujaq

Sanikiluaq

NEWFOUNDLAND
and LABRADOR

Kuujjuaraapik

ANITOBA   ONTARIO   James   QUÉBEC
                                  Bay

Acknowledgements

The massive collection created by Jerry Twomey is significant not only for its aesthetic breadth but also for the detailed research that he carried out and carefully documented throughout the years. His interest in the individuals who created the art will be a lasting contribution to our knowledge of Inuit creativity in the 1950s and 1960s. However, I felt that it was important to document some of the information that existed in Jerry Twomey's mind and memory as well. This was much to ask after an interval of 30-40 years, and I would like to extend my appreciation to him for his patience and his time as I probed his memory on several occasions, in 1997, 1999, 2002, and 2003. He gave generously of his time when he travelled to Winnipeg to visit his family.

I would like to thank Richard Murdoch of La Fédération des Co-opératives du Nouveau Québec for facilitating copyright permissions for Nunavik communities and Terry Ryan for this assistance for Cape Dorset. R. J. Ramrattan of Canadian Arctic Producers gave valued assistance obtaining copyright permissions from artists and co-operatives in Nunavut communities other than Cape Dorset. Mercy Kayuryuk provided this service for Baker Lake.

I would like to thank Ginny Twomey for her help with the public event honouring her uncle held at the Gallery on December 10, 2003. My thanks also go to all Winnipeg Art Gallery staff who helped to make this exhibition and catalogue possible, particularly our photographer, Ernest Mayer, and the Installations team headed by Carey Archibald.

Darlene Coward Wight

Copyright Permissions

All Nunavik sculptures are reproduced with the permission of La Fédération des Coopératives du Nouveau-Québec. Cape Dorset sculpture reproduced with the permission of West Baffin Eskimo Co-operative. All other permissions are courtesy of the artists, with the assistance of the following co-operatives: Kimik Co-operative Association, Kissarvik Co-operative Association, Mitiq Co-operative Association, Naujat Co-operative Association, Padlei Co-operative Association, Pangnirtung Eskimo Co-operative, Taqqut Co-operative Limited.

Credits

Photography of artwork and Jerry Twomey: Ernest Mayer

Photography of artists: Jerry Twomey

Catalogue design: Frank Reimer

Editing: Jenny Gates

Copy Editing: Heather Mousseau

Pre-press and printing: Friesens Corporation

Generous sponsorship for this exhibition was received from Friesens Corporation and The Volunteer Committee to The Winnipeg Art Gallery.

THE WINNIPEG ART GALLERY
Involving People In The Visual Arts

300 Memorial Blvd. Winnipeg, Manitoba R3C 1V1
Tel.: (204) 786-6641 WAG ArtSite: www.wag.mb.ca